GOD IS FOR
THE ALCOHOLIC

GOD IS FOR
THE ALCOHOLIC

By

JERRY G. DUNN

MOODY PRESS
CHICAGO

Moody Paperback Edition, 1967

Library of Congress Catalog Card Number: 65-24232

© 1965 by The Moody Bible Institute of Chicago

Affordable Version, 1984
ISBN 0-8024-2138-5
1 2 3 4 5 6 7 Printing/LC/Year 89 88 87 86 85 84

Printed in the United States of America

CONTENTS

Part I

UNDERSTANDING ALCOHOLISM

Part II

FIVE WAYS TO HELP THE ALCOHOLIC

Part III

FIVE WAYS THE ALCOHOLIC CAN HELP HIMSELF

DEDICATION

To my dear wife, Greta,
who stood by and believed God,
trusting Him to set me free

ACKNOWLEDGMENT

My thanks to my good friend, Bernard Palmer,
Christian author, without whose assistance I
could not have written this book.

Part I

UNDERSTANDING ALCOHOLISM

INTRODUCTION

GOD IS FOR THE ALCOHOLIC! I discovered that for myself at the conclusion of a two-year drunk when I picked up a Bible in my cell in a Texas prison more than sixteen years ago. I have seen it proved over and over again in the lives of men and women in every stratum of our society. There is hope for the alcoholic and his bewildered, suffering family. But alcoholism is such a confusing and complex problem that many of God's children do not know how to be used of Him in helping the alcoholic.

In these pages we hope to be able to give a little better understanding of the problem, the product, and the person of the alcoholic. We hope to show how, under the direction of God, this helpless individual can be intelligently aided.

1

UNDERSTANDING THE PROBLEM

ONE OF THE DIFFICULTIES in understanding and treating the alcoholic is the complexity of the problem. We probe for the reasons a man is in the condition he is in, and we overlook the fact of addiction. I feel we should accept addiction to alcohol as the reason, and start the road of recovery from there.

Not long ago, in one of the group therapy classes in our New Life Program,* the problem of alcohol addiction was being discussed. Each of the forty-five men present gave a different reason for his own addiction to alcohol.

"I suppose you could say I drink because I'm lonely," one man said. "Usually when I go into a bar, it's not for liquor. I just want to find someone to talk to. But the first thing I know I've got a glass in my hand, and I'm 'gone' again."

"I used to want to be somebody and make something of my life," another told us. "But I just didn't have what it takes. I've always been a failure, and I suppose I'll always be one."

"I've been a drunk for more than twenty years," still another admitted candidly. "Before I came here to the mission I didn't even try to get help. The way I saw it, there

*Rehabilitation program of the Open Door Mission, Omaha, Nebraska.

wasn't any use. A guy like me could never learn to live without alcohol."

What these men said is what I have found to be typical of alcoholics. They have their problems all figured out. They reach the conclusion it is hopeless to try to change.

Had we accepted the reasons these men gave as causes we would have been faced with a staggering number of problems that would have defied solution. We would have been just as helpless to point them to a life of sobriety as they were helpless to free themselves from alcoholism.

But when they were confronted with the facts that people can become addicted to beverage alcohol, they began to understand their own behavior. They began to see that their strange pattern of living was developed to satisfy their addictive drive and did not necessarily come from a personality defect. Hope of taking their places as useful, upright members of society was thus seen as within their reach.

This thought does not agree with a popular present-day concept which sets forth the theory that a person is an alcoholic due to a physical, moral, or psychological defect in his makeup. Due to this defect, the theory maintains, a person was an alcoholic even before he took his first drink. This thinking takes all blame from alcoholic beverages and places it on the individual.

The fact that there are those who drink because of such defects cannot be denied. Yet basic research does not hold to the premise that the psychological makeup of a man is the primary cause of his addiction to alcohol.

Dr. Robert Flemming, one of the leaders in the World Health Organization, says, "Most alcoholics are not psychiatric cases; they are normal people." The conclusion reached in a fifty-six-page report issued by the World Health Organization is: "First, nobody is immune to alcoholism. Second, total abstinence is the only solution." The report opened with this statement: "Alcohol is a poison to the nervous system. The double solubility of alcohol in water and fat enables it to invade the nerve cell. A man may become a chronic alcoholic without ever having shown symptoms of drunkenness."

In studies conducted by Dr. Edwin H. Sunderland of Indiana University, the same conclusion was reached. "He, the alcoholic, could be a sad type, or a happy type, an introvert or an extrovert. In short, he could be anybody."

Thus we see that alcoholism starts with the social drinking of alcoholic beverages, not with a problem personality. To understand this, we must know that the alcoholic content of all alcoholic beverages—wine, beer, whiskey—is made up of ethyl alcohol, a habit-forming drug.

Dr. Andrew C. Ivy, formerly head of the Clinical Science Department of the University of Illinois, has this to say about the subject: "Beverage alcohol is an intoxicating, hypnotic analgesic, an anesthetic narcotic, poisonous and potentially habit-forming, craving-producing or addiction-producing drug or chemical."

The late Dr. E. M. Jellinek,* one of the world's leading authorities on the subjects of alcohol and alcoholism, had much to say about alcohol addiction.

Before quoting the findings of twenty-two studies on the subject, covering a period from 1935-1960, Dr. Jellinek wrote, "Most of these formulations will come as a shock to those who believe in the obsolescence of the idea of alcoholism as a true addiction and who do not recognize that alcohol itself plays more of a role in the process of alcoholism than just that of causing intoxication."

*Dr. E. M. Jellinek was founder of the Yale Center of Alcohol Studies, the Yale Summer School of Alcohol Studies, the Yale Plan Clinics, the Classified Abstract Archive of the Alcohol Literature, and the Master Bibliography of Alcohol Literature. He was also the cofounder of the National Council on Alcoholism and has been the World Health Organization Consultant on Alcoholism.

Dr. Jellinek quotes Adams as writing in 1935, "Alcohol is one of the addiction producing drugs."

In 1954 Pohlisch said, "The process of alcohol addiction is comparable to the pharmacalogical processes operative in all drug addictions."

In 1956 Pfeffer was a little more specific. "Loss of control over the use of alcohol, change in tolerance, a withdrawal syndrome and the relinquishing of all other interests in favor of a preoccupation with the use of alcohol are all criteria of an addiction."

The *Journal of the American Medical Association* published a series of articles on alcoholism (completed in 1957) prepared by members of the Committee on Alcoholism of the AMA's Council on Mental Health. They make a distinction between alcoholics, and divide them into two groups. The first, primary alcoholics, are those who become slaves to ethyl alcohol because of addiction. Secondary alcoholics are those who at first drink compulsively because of personal problems or for physical reasons.

Among the *primary alcoholics* probably the most pitiable is the individual who is attracted to alcohol from the very first drink and keeps right on drinking until he is a slave to it.

The wife of a prominent person in our community belongs to that group. At a cocktail party she was induced to take a drink for the first time, at the age of fifty-seven.

She came home and told her husband, "I didn't know what I'd been missing. I'll never be without alcohol as long as I live."

She started drinking and continued to drink compulsively, and now she lives just for the bottle.

A man in Chicago, relating his story, told how he was raised in a Christian home, taught Sunday school, and studied for the ministry. "You may find this hard to believe," he said, "but I had never taken a drink or smoked a cigarette until I was in my twenties. Then I took one drink and—*boom!* I was drunk more than I was sober. I plunged to the bottom in a matter of weeks and went from one skid row to another up and down the country for ten solid years until the Lord got hold of me again."

The AMA report also deals with the individual who drinks regularly over a period of years until he develops such a craving for alcohol that he cannot leave it alone. He is the person who started by drinking socially, got into the habit, and finally came to the place where he is addicted to alcohol.

Studies made by Dr. Jellinek conclude that addiction sets in after a period of seven years of regular drinking. Surveys made by Alcoholics Anonymous have found that after seven to twelve years of regular drinking many drinkers become alcoholics.

The term "alcoholism" was first used by Magnus Huss and may be defined as any change in the condition of the body or in its physical or mental activities caused by ethyl alcohol or alcoholic beverages. Alcoholism is literally a poisoning by spirits, and the most common symptoms are toxemia and paralysis.

It is the ethyl alcohol in beer, whiskey and other liquors that causes intoxication. It is ethyl alcohol that causes addiction.

The fact that most people don't recognize the addictive qualities of beverage alcohol is the principal reason social drinking is so dangerous. They don't know what the results of a seemingly harmless activity can be until it is too late.

A small town businessman came to our office for help with a serious drinking problem some months ago. Recently his wife admitted that she was the one who first urged him to drink. And for social reasons.

"Everyone in our crowd drank at parties and at our bridge club," she said. "I felt stupid asking for a Coke or 7-up when everyone else had a martini. So I told him that no harm could come of taking one drink with the others."

She was aware of no harm until, with the horrifying impact of a bomb explosion, she saw that her husband was addicted to alcohol.

"We live in a drinking society," said Miss Phyllis Snyder, Executive Director of the Alcoholic Treatment Center in Chicago, "and therefore society is responsible for the problem involved therewith. When I was a girl, guests in a home were usually served coffee. Now, as soon as they arrive the host asks, 'How about a drink?'"

Pressure is constantly put upon people to drink to be sociable. With the increase of drinking, addiction increases.

The amount of drinking done by women has risen rapidly. Cocktail parties are taking the place of afternoon coffee parties and liquor is more and more often served at bridge clubs. Some drink because they have a great deal of leisure and are bored. Some drink because it has become the thing to do in their circle of society. But, whatever the reason, addiction starts with social drinking. The results are just what one would expect. An article in the January, 1962 issue of the *Saturday Evening Post* estimated that half of the known alcoholics in the United States are women.

One of the problems of working with the alcoholic is this increase in the popularity of social drinking. As we study the problem of beverage alcohol, we more clearly understand the Bible verse, "Wine is a mocker, strong drink is raging: and whosoever is deceived thereby is not wise" (Proverbs 20:1).

The time was when a man was judged as intoxicated or sober by his ability to walk straight and to speak distinctly. That is no longer the case.

Dr. Harvey Wiley said it this way. "A man can be intoxicated without tottering or without disclosing in any way to the ordinary sense the fact that he is intoxicated."

Dr. Yendell Henderson, Professor of Applied Psychology at Yale University, said, "Since the introduction of the automobile, however, the definition [of intoxication] may be changed to that which appreciably impairs the ability of a man or a woman to drive an automobile with safety to the general public."

Dr. Morris Fishbein wrote his own convictions on the same subject in the AMA Journal. "Just a drink or two and the safe driver is turned into a reckless traffic menace."

There is good reason for this. Ethyl alcohol, when taken into the body, goes almost immediately into the blood stream and up to the brain. It begins to affect the cortex of the brain, where the higher brain centers that have to do with memory, conscience, and judgment are located. The anesthetic effect of alcohol slows man's reactions measurably. It decreases his ability to judge distances and to tell the difference between visual and auditory stimulae.

It adversely affects skilled performance. A crack rifle team discovered that so little as a glass of beer materially lowered their scores.

But that is not all. Ethyl alcohol makes it more difficult to memorize data and solve problems.

Those who drink will argue that while drinking may affect the driving ability of others it does not affect them. However, tests conducted by the University of Washington School of Medicine give the lie to that opinion. They discovered that only 3/100 percent of ethyl alcohol in the blood stream lowered a person's driving efficiency by 25 percent. Two cans of beer or its equivalent will produce this effect in the individual of average size. Increase the alcoholic intake to six cans of beer, and the individual will have 10/100 percent of alcohol in his blood stream and his ability to drive will be retarded by 85 percent.

There is no arguing with the evidence, especially since it is corroborated by no less an authority than the National Safety Council. They speak in grim statistics. They say that 50 percent of all traffic deaths are caused by drinking drivers. Twenty thousand persons die and four hundred thousand are injured annually in accidents caused by drinking drivers.

There are an estimated eight million known alcoholics in America. Dr. Andrew Ivy notes their numbers are increasing by four hundred and fifty thousand each year. A survey of divorce cases in courts reveals that 60 percent of all divorces have drinking in their background. The increase in the numbers of illegitimate births each year is parallel with the increased consumption of alcoholic beverages among young people. And in the field of crime 75 percent of all crimes are committed by those under the influence of alcohol.

"Radioactive fallout may pose a health menace to Americans," Dr. Ivy concluded, "but alcoholism is a more serious one."

I believe the Bible clearly teaches that the problem is with the product, not the individual: "Who hath woe? who hath sorrow? who hath contentions? who hath babbling? who hath wounds without cause? who hath redness of eyes? They that tarry long at the wine; they that go to seek mixed wine. . . . At the last it biteth like a serpent, and stingeth like an adder" (Proverbs 23:29-32).

The secondary alcoholic, according to the AMA use of the term, is an entirely different type of individual than the primary alcoholic. The secondary alcoholic is trying to escape from his personal problems by hiding in the bottle.

That category is the one into which I fitted, at least partially. I started drinking conventionally enough, using it as a sales tool in the advertising and sales promotion business.

When I experienced a few business reversals, I remembered the way a cocktail had relaxed me, so I began to drink because I was tense and worried. It wasn't long until I was addicted.

An older man we'll call John was another fellow who drank because of a personal problem. He didn't drink at all until after his wife died. Left with four small children and a limited income that made it all but impossible to hire a housekeeper, he saw no way to turn—except to alcohol. Beverage alcohol had a numbing effect on John's mind and made it possible for him to forget his troubles for a few hours. If he got drunk enough he could temporarily forget that his children were in foster homes.

John's bouts with the bottle only increased his problems, which in turn caused him to drink more often. First he lost his job. Next, he lost his home. Then, in addition to his personal troubles, before he even realized what was happening, he was caught in the savage vice of alcohol addiction.

The guilt complex can play a big part in sending the secondary alcoholic on the downward road of alcoholism. For instance, a young man came to us for help who admitted he was an alcoholic and wanted to be set free. He had a good background, was well educated with an outstanding ability as a private secretary. He had held such a position with a leading businessman and civic leader. Under the influence of alcoholic beverages this young man had committed a crime that placed him in prison for two years. Because of his ability and fine family background everyone wanted to help him make a new start. But he could not maintain any degree of success for any length of time. Just as he would reach his goal, he would go on another drunk. Prayerful study of his problem showed he had a guilt complex he could not overcome. He felt he did not deserve success because he had disgraced his family.

The secondary alcoholic may have a physical problem—

rather than a psychological one—that causes him to drink compulsively.

A nervous, sensitive person, Steve stuttered terribly. As an impressionable boy, however, he discovered that it didn't hurt so much when people laughed at him if he had had a drink or two. In fact, liquor loosed his inhibitions until he could make sport of the infirmity that hurt so much when he was sober. His drinking soon caused addiction, a fact that was aggravated by a stretch in the army during the Korean police action. After losing his wife and family and everything he considered worth living for, he continued to drink heavily until ethyl alcohol finally took his life.

Another such individual came into my office not long ago. "Liquor has complete control over me," he admitted miserably.

"What is your problem as far as alcohol is concerned?" I asked him.

"That's just it. As far as I know I don't have any personal problems that would cause me to drink the way I do. My business is good, and we're not in any financial difficulties. I have a fine wife and family, and we get along very well together. I don't have any problems at all except," he said sheepishly, "that I can't sleep at night. I've got undulant fever, and insomnia seems to go with it."

This was his problem, although he did not realize it. He wouldn't be able to sleep for several nights in a row. Tension would begin to build. Then he would drink liquor so he could sleep. He soon became addicted to alcohol, as did the man who stuttered. The weakness that caused him to begin to drink regularly was soon succeeded by the greater weakness of his insatiable, acquired thirst for ethyl alcohol.

There are social, psychological, and physiological reasons why a man becomes an alcoholic, but there is still one underlying cause.

Howard Whitman, a well known science writer, published a series of articles in the *Des Moines Register* under the title "Our Drinking Habits." After reviewing the subject thoroughly in twelve installments, he made this final statement, "Alcoholism emerges as a sickness of the soul."

Alcoholism is a sickness of the soul—a sin sickness, and it must be considered such.

2

THE START OF SEVEN STEPS DOWN

BEFORE IT IS POSSIBLE to help the alcoholic, it is necessary to understand him. In doing that we must remember that all alcoholism starts with social drinking.

"Even though I know you don't drink, even socially," a medical doctor told a friend of ours, "you may be an alcoholic."

While we might question the doctor's terminology, what he said could in a general way be true. The fellow may be psychotic. He may be neurotic. He may have some other type of personality difficulty that would make him particularly vulnerable to alcohol addiction. He might even be the type of person who has only to take one drink to ignite the flames of thirst that would destroy him.

But, until he takes that first drink he is as safe from alcoholic addiction as Adam and Eve were safe from death before they ate of the fruit of the tree of knowledge of good and evil.

There are seven distinct, well-defined steps downward from sobriety to alcoholism and complete deterioration of the human mind and body. In the life of any given individual, some of the steps may be blurred and tend to run into one another, but careful examination will reveal each of them.

They can be warning signals—stop signs in the progressive downward march to alcoholism and destruction by it, or they can be signposts to mark the distance a man has yet to go. Unfortunately, his loved ones cannot decide which they will be in any given case. Only the individual himself can make such a decision.

The first step is social drinking. Practically without exception, people start to drink because someone offers them a drink.

High school fellows or girls may take a first drink for fear of being laughed at by the crowd, or to prove that they are adult, or simply out of curiosity. A good many take their first drink of alcoholic beverages during the celebration following a junor-senior prom, or during or after a graduation-night party.

In college, social affairs get more important and frequent, and liquor begins to take a more prominent role in them.

"You have to drink a little," a university sophomore said. "Everybody does."

The pattern for so-called gracious living includes drinking. The "hospitality hour" and the cocktail party become an accepted part of social life. Even the young person with convictions against drinking is under powerful, though subtle, pressures to join the crowd.

At many parties the pressure to get everyone to drink is so great that it seems almost necessary for a guest to have a glass in his hand, even though it contains only ginger ale. Anything to make the others feel more comfortable.

"I don't know why people will come to our neighborhood parties and be so smug they won't drink," a woman complained in Ann Landers' column. "It wouldn't hurt them to take just one cocktail."

"The more education an American has, the more likely he

is to drink," says Robert W. Jones, assistant director of the Center of Alcohol Studies at Rutgers University.

"More than half the people with only an elementary education drink," he said. "Approximately 70 percent of those with high school educations drink, while the percentage is greater among college graduates."

According to *Contact* magazine,* the liquor industry spends a colossal 400 million dollars a year in radio, newspaper, magazine, and television advertising. Their purpose is to cloak their product with some semblance of respectability and to foster the notion that for a social occasion to be successful some form of alcoholic beverage must be served.

No one, when he is starting to drink, wants to become a slave to beverage alcohol. He doesn't want to drink until he staggers or makes a fool of himself. He doesn't want to make a liquor bottle the first love of his life—to the exclusion of his family, his friends, and his job. He reasons, "That isn't going to happen to me." He feels he is too smart to let liquor get control of him. He has too much willpower, too much self-control. The chances are that he will not even recognize the danger signals until it is too late.

Although social drinking is the first step to alcoholism, another, even more insidious, danger is the idea, rapidly taking hold of more and more people, that to demonstrate hospitality an alcoholic beverage must be served. Social drinking is the snare that traps many individuals who have fought their way back to sobriety.

A man we'll call Pete was such a person. The path had been long and difficult for him, but at last he had reached the place where he could stay sober. He won back his wife and family, got a good job, bought a new home, and was getting ahead again. It had been five years since he had had a drink.

*Issue of February 1, 1960, p. 10. Published twice monthly by the Methodist Episcopal Church.

Then his wife went to visit her mother, and while he was staying at home alone the people in the block had a house-warming on a new couple who had moved into the neighborhood. Anxious to be hospitable, the newcomers brought a case of beer from the basement.

Pete hesitated a little. How could he explain to complete strangers that he didn't drink? How could he go into an embarrassing explanation of the reason why? These were his thoughts. So he took a glass of beer.

The fires of alcoholism had not been put out. They had only been banked within him, and were still smoldering. The taste of alcohol in that single glass of beer was enough to send them racing out of control.

Although five years had elapsed, he started to drink again. You know the rest of the story. He lost his job, his home, his family, and he finally hit skid row. All because someone offered him a social drink of beverage alcohol.

The second step down is dependent drinking. The alcoholic's reasons for drinking change subtly but perceptibly. No longer does he drink only when he has guests or is a guest himself. He becomes either a *habit drinker* or a *dependent drinker*. Which type he is depends upon his reason for drinking in the first place. It depends upon whether he could be considered by the AMA classification as a primary or secondary alcoholic.

The *habit drinker* is the fellow who is just beginning to feel the powerful, insistent tug of addiction. He mixes a drink when he comes home from the office, or after dinner while he is reading or watching television. He probably doesn't even realize that his habitual drinking can lead him to alcoholism.

"It became a regular ritual with us," said one young woman whose marriage was threatened because her husband was an alcoholic. "At first, we only drank socially. Then about once or twice a week Paul would mix us a drink as soon as he got home from work. It wasn't long until he went from the hall closet where he hung his coat and hat directly to the kitchen to mix a drink. Still, neither one of us thought anything about it."

The *dependent drinker* drinks when things start to build up, when the problems get too great for him. His boss chews him out on the job; he loses a big contract; his wife wants to spend more than he thinks they can afford on new furniture; or a bill collector gets nasty. So he drinks. It helps him to forget what has happened. The disappointments and frustrations don't seem to be so great under the temporary glow produced by beverage alcohol.

I know quite a lot about that sort of drinking. I used to do my share of it, so my knowledge is firsthand.

If something happened that disturbed me or made me angry I'd head for the nearest bar or package store. That the bottle never solved a single problem of mine never occurred to me. Nor did I face the fact that I always felt worse and less able to cope with life when the effect of the liquor wore off than I had before I took the drink. Even though at that time my chief compulsion to drink came from the pressures I faced, I was becoming addicted to ethyl alcohol. And, like the habit drinker, I didn't even realize it.

There is little difference, actually, between the *habit drinker* and the *dependent drinker*. Both are in the early stages of alcohol addiction.

The third step down is the prealcoholic phase. Here, again, the step is sharply defined. Well entrenched now as a regular drinker of alcoholic beverages, the individual begins to drink hastily. He begins to gulp his drinks, to drink on the sly, to sneak drinks. At a party, he's the bighearted guy who wants to be the bartender.

On one pretext or another the fellow in the prealcoholic

phase will manage to get out into the kitchen to mix drinks. His own glass is always filled to the brim, or perhaps he'll make and gulp down an extra one every time he mixes a drink for someone else. Although up until this point he may seldom have shown the effects of drinking too much, he now begins to reveal evidence of intoxication at otherwise quiet cocktail parties.

"I'll never forget the first time my husband actually drank too much that I knew about," a distraught wife confided in me. "We had gone to a New Year's Eve party at a friend's home. The other guests had two or three drinks, but Herman must have had one every time he went to the kitchen. He made a fool of himself at the party and fell on the floor twice before I got him home and to bed."

Herman said he felt terrible about his exhibition and swore off liquor—for a whole week.

"It seemed, after that," she went on, "that at every third or fourth cocktail party we went to he got in that condition." Tears came to her eyes. "He certainly isn't like the man I married."

She spoke the truth. He wasn't the same man she had married twelve or fourteen years before. A change in his personality had set in. He had begun to develop what is known as an alcoholic personality.

"He never used to lie to me," she went on. "It didn't make any difference what had happened, or how angry the truth made me, he had never lied to me—but I began to catch him telling me things that weren't true. I soon found out that I couldn't believe anything he said."

Herman would call his wife, very apologetically, to tell her that a deal demanded his immediate attention. "I don't know what's the matter with people that they can't conduct business at a decent hour," he would tell her, "but a good customer called a few minutes ago and insisted that I make a presentation to him and the assistant purchasing agent before they go to New York tonight. I tried every way I know to get out of it, but it's either do as they say or lose the order."

When he told such lies, he sounded very convincing, even when he would be gone all night. One time his car broke down and he was so far out in the country he had to wait until morning to get help. He had told his secretary to phone and tell his wife he'd been called to a neighboring town unexpectedly and probably wouldn't be able to get home that night. His excuses were very plausible and convincing.

Even in the prealcoholic phase the individual becomes an accomplished liar. Deceit and lying become a way of life to him as he seeks to keep his family and his employer from knowing that he is drinking more and more.

This is something you must remember if you are dealing with an alcoholic. It doesn't make any difference who he is. It doesn't make any difference whether he is rich or poor, intelligent or not so intelligent, important or unimportant, in the course of becoming addicted to alcohol, the individual becomes a very accomplished liar. He is able to look you straight in the eye and speak with the tones of one taking a solemn oath without uttering a single word of truth.

The fourth step down is problem drinking. This is the phase where the prealcoholic drinker begins to lose control of his drinking habits. Up until this time, he could control the time he started to drink and the time he stopped. Now he has reached the stage when he can control the time he starts to drink, but he can't stop when he wants to. The fires of alcohol addiction begin to flame higher, and he can no longer quench his thirst, once it has been aroused by alcoholic beverages. He begins to go on weekend drunks.

A fellow we'll call Ken was like this. A near genius mechanically, he and a partner had developed a piece of equipment that could be used by large contractors. They began to manufacture it and set out to contact prospective customers.

"Ken would spend weeks setting up the appointments," a disturbed employee confided. "He'd take money he needed badly for pressing bills and go to a place like Chicago or Philadelphia or New York to see important buyers. Then, to bolster his courage, he'd take a drink. He'd get stinking drunk and lie in his hotel room for two or three days, missing all his appointments."

Ross H— had a similar problem. He was the vice-president in charge of sales for a nationally distributed product. It was his responsibility to train and encourage district sales managers across the country. All such sales meetings included a hospitality hour, which he would arrange and supervise.

At first, Ross was able to take a drink or leave it alone. It was a part of his job—social drinking. It wasn't long until he was drinking habitually and was only a step from the pre-alcoholic phase. When he came to that phase he drank more than anyone else at the party. Then, without quite realizing what had happened, he came to the place where he could no longer stop drinking when he wanted to.

He would arrange for the area sales force to come into a central location, and would have every intention of carrying out the elaborate program he had set up. But at the hospitality hour he would drink so much he was unable to conduct the meeting. He not only made a fool of himself but word got around that he ruined his sales meetings by his drinking. After two or three warnings, he lost his position—one that paid him an annual salary in five figures.

The loss of his job meant real problems for Ross at home and with his friends, including a personality change which is typical of the problem drinker as he progresses downward. He began to become dependent upon others as fears and anxiety set in. What a change was seen in this man who had been such a dynamic individual as he fought his way to the top of his department! Supremely confident of his own ability, Ross had waded into any task that was given him with a strong determination to see it through. Now the very qualities which had first attracted the attention of the top management and gained him rapid advancement had gradually faded away.

Another man who became a problem drinker frequently went to bridge or cocktail parties with his wife on Saturday nights. Once in a while they went somewhere with friends for an entire weekend. The husband's drinking soon became a serious problem.

"I can't understand it," his wife said. "When Don takes a drink, it seems as though he can't stop. Last Saturday night he got drunk and wasn't sober until Monday morning."

It wasn't long until he was staying drunk well into the next week. His wife felt that she had to cover up for him in order to help him keep from losing his job.

"Don's sick this morning," she would tell the supervisor. "He has the flu." Or, "There's something wrong with his back. I've been trying to get him to see the doctor."

A once competent, self-assured workman, Don depended upon his wife to lie for him when he got drunk and to help him keep the truth from his employer. He began to realize that he had a problem with alcoholic beverages—a real problem, and he was caught between savage fear and pride on one hand and the gradual realization of his true situation on the other.

It is at this point that the problem drinker experiences great torment. He goes somewhere to do a job and starts to drink and he can't stop. He becomes dead drunk. Only vaguely does he remember anything that happened.

I shall never forget the torment I found myself in as I left a midwest town one time when I was in this stage of alcoholism. The past several days were a complete blank. I had no idea what had happened, except that I knew I had written checks all over that town and didn't have the money to cover them.

I began to see that I was a liar, a cheat, a thief, and a drunkard. I wouldn't have admitted any of those things to anyone else, but deep in my own heart I knew they were true. It was a frightening experience. Believe me.

"If I could just take care of the immediate problem," I reasoned, "I can handle things from here on. If I could just get enough money to make those checks good, I won't get myself into a mess like that again." Yet the gnawing realization that I was helpless against the fierce thirst that was taking hold of me was a real torment.

Frantically, I began to search for answers, but all the time I was fearful that people would find me out. I will never forget how eagerly I went to that psychiatrist a short time later and how desperate I was for help. But pride wouldn't let me admit that I needed help. Pride wouldn't let me admit to anyone that I had a problem with beverage alcohol.

From this point, the progression downward for the alcoholic almost becomes a rush.

3

THE END THEREOF

The fifth step down is the dropover into alcoholism itself. Until he reaches this point the problem drinker is able to maintain a somewhat normal life. His growing addiction to alcohol is now affecting members of his family, his friends, and associates.

He reaches the place where his entire life is centered around one thing, and only one thing—getting another drink. He can no longer control either the time he starts drinking or the time he stops drinking.

Even though he may want—desperately—to keep from drinking, his very being screams for the alcohol to which he has become addicted. He starts to drink because he cannot help it, and he continues to drink in long periods of intoxication because he cannot keep from it.

His body has built up a dependence upon alcohol that cannot be denied. His entire existence becomes a battle to satisfy this insatiable craving for alcohol. He becomes crafty almost to the point of animal cunning.

For instance, one alcoholic I know had a kennel of hunting dogs in his backyard. Let the dogs bark, which they usually did several times during an evening, and he would have to go out to see what was wrong. He had bottles stashed in the garage, in a pair of breast waders hanging in the back entryway, and in a host of other places. He could go anywhere on his property and the chances were that he wouldn't be any more than forty feet from a quick drink.

After his conversion to Christ and complete deliverance from the power of alcohol he laughingly told me about finding bottles in the most surprising places.

"For six months after I quit drinking," he said, "we kept turning up liquor every time we moved a piece of canvas or opened a toolbox or cleaned the garage. To tell you the truth, I didn't even remember hiding most of it."

You see, the alcoholic finally reaches the place where his dependence upon alcohol is so complete that he is terrified at the thought of needing a drink and not being able to get it.

Another characteristic of the dropover into alcoholism is the individual's attitude toward his job. The average alcoholic is an exceptional workman. Whatever his responsibilities at work, they will be carried out very acceptably.

Strangely enough, this also is a part of the pattern. It marks another step downward in the progression to alcoholism. The trouble is in his motive. He may or may not be either ambitious or conscientious when he is sober. But now he works well because of fear.

You see, in the back of his mind he knows that, sooner or later, he's going to get drunk and not be able to get back to work on Monday or Tuesday. He's afraid that when the inevitable happens, he'll be let out—unless he has made an outstanding work record. So, he works as hard as he can to make himself so valuable to the firm for whom he works that they won't fire him.

Another fear can motivate him to work exceptionally hard. He knows that when he has been on drunks before he has done things that he would never have done had he been sober. Perhaps he wrote bad checks or gambled or walked off without paying a hotel bill, or had a close brush with jail or the penitentiary. He thinks that if he works hard enough—or, if he's a salesman and has a high enough record of sales—the company will stand him. If they like him well enough, they may advance him enough money to get things straightened out.

The alcoholic, you must remember, is cunning. He's always thinking ahead. He's always trying to prepare for the unexpected. He realizes his own weaknesses, although he won't admit them, and is constantly trying to hedge against their getting him into a corner.

We often find this trait among the men at the Mission. An employer hires a fellow from us. From the very first he becomes the best dishwasher or ditchdigger or dockman the firm has ever had. He works hard without complaining and does his work so well his employer can't help being favorably impressed. After a few days the new man goes to the boss.

"I haven't been able to take care of my room rent," he will lie, "and the landlady has given me until tonight to get the money. I wonder if I could get a little advance on my wages?"

The employer is usually so glad to have a new man who works so well he doesn't mind letting him have a few dollars. With money in his pocket, the fellow almost runs over somebody getting to the nearest bar, where he proceeds to get drunk. That's the last his employer ever sees of him.

Although the individual in this stage works well, his motive is entirely selfish. All his thoughts and desires are directed toward getting another drink. In this phase of his downward trend we see the complete change in his personality.

When a person is in the prealcoholic phase he starts lying. When he becomes a problem drinker, he begins to develop a dependence upon other people and is beset by the torment of fear and anxiety. He is but a short step away from alcoholism. When he drops over into alcohol addiction, his personality change is complete.

He not only lies and deceives everyone around him but he becomes self-centered and antisocial. He doesn't want to be around people—especially strangers. He would rather miss a meal than sit down to a table with others, and will often keep crackers and cheese or canned food in his room, so he can eat alone.

He won't make decisions, and he becomes dependent upon his wife, his family, and perhaps the entire community.

But paradoxically, he is proud—so proud he will cling to any illusion that will keep people from finding out what he is really like.

For instance, one competent wood-carver at the Chicago Christian Industrial League did some beautiful carvings but refused to show them or to sell them. Charles Morey, former superintendent of the League, said, "He's put himself into those carvings, but pride keeps him from showing them."

The alcoholic is often far too proud to allow his wife and children to draw relief of any kind, yet he is very willing to live off his wife's earnings.

The wife of an alcoholic shoe salesman came to see me some time ago. She brought up, among other things, the matter of her working. "We have four small children, and I feel that I should be home with them," she said. "We could live quite comfortably on my husband's income, but he flies into a rage if I even mention giving up my job and staying at home."

In such a situation, the typical alcoholic wants his wife to keep on working because in the corner of his mind is the nagging fear that one of these days he's going to get into financial trouble because of his drinking and will need the income from her job to fall back on.

Another young man I knew was even more dependent upon his wife. Acute alcoholism took his life a short time ago, but while he lived he was satisfied to let his wife (the mother of two small children) work to support the family and him.

In this phase of his descent into alcoholism the individual will probably lose his job because of his drinking. Of one thing, however, we can be sure. Unless someone gets hold of him and presents the claims of Christ on his life and helps him intelligently with his problem, it won't be the last job alcohol will cost him.

The man in an average home situation is the one who is apt to develop a dependency upon his family. The homeless man often develops a dependency upon society.

One skid-row character in a Midwestern city spent 312 days out of the past year in jail. The charge was always the same—drunkenness. Jail was a way of life to him. It meant warmth, food, and a place to sleep at night—in a way, a measure of security.

For other alcoholics, the cycle is more complex but is for the same purpose. They go from jail to the hospital to the rescue mission to an alcoholic rehabilitation center and back to the jail again.

The matter of the alcoholic's dependence upon others presents one of the most difficult and serious problems a counselor or family faces in working with the alcoholic. Dependence upon others must be broken before the alcoholic can be helped. This we will consider more extensively in the chapter on counseling.

The sixth step down is the subtle descent into chronic alcoholism.

While the plunge from problem drinking to alcoholism is sudden and marked, the drift into *chronic alcoholism* is gradual. After losing one job because of his drinking, the individual gets another job. For a time all seems to go well. Then his drinking puts him out of work again.

Tom was like that. An expert in the field of electronics, he was able to get work quite easily. He drifted from Kansas to Minnesota to Florida and back to Kansas on one job after another, taking his family with him. Each new start looked promising. In each job he was given advancements and raises for the excellence of his work. He was finally fired from each job for the same reason—his excessive drinking.

Each time Tom took a job in a new community, he was determined that things were going to be different. He had left all of his old friends behind. He wasn't going to run with a drinking crowd any more. And for a while things would appear to be better, but he began to drink again. He drank away a good home and furniture and a late model car. The last move he and his wife made, they had enough money for a bus ticket halfway across the country to a place where he was going to make another new start, and all the clothes they owned were in a single suitcase.

Tom is very much like an engineer I knew who was very competent and could find work with ease. Even after he got to drinking so heavily that he lost his job, he could still go to another company and get work. Finally, however, the whole engineering profession put a black mark against him. Knowing that he was a poor work risk, management refused to hire him anywhere in his chosen profession.

However, he had something else to fall back on. As a young man in school he had worked for an uncle who was a caterer. When work in engineering was no longer available to him, he became a cook, an expert baker, and a kitchen manager. He would work in a café or bakery until the owner got tired of his drunkenness and fired him. Since there is always a shortage of cooks and bakers, he could move on, finding a little work for another bottle. All the while the bands of alcohol addiction were becoming a little tighter.

At this stage of chronic alcoholism, the individual's family and friends have become so disgusted and heartsick they have finally turned against him. He is very much alone.

The pattern continues with his going on a long period of intoxication, which finally ends in delirium tremens. By this time, he is no stranger to the inside of jails and has a resigned, passive attitude toward being arrested, as though there is no shame to it. While his twisted pride remains, his self-respect is all but gone. It is during this phase that he will probably be hospitalized for the first time because of his drinking.

He is almost at the bottom.

The seventh step down is organic deterioration.

He has reached the place where he no longer cares how he looks. He is dirty and unshaven. His eyes are bleary, and his face is perpetually bloated and flushed.

No longer is he a good worker in order to cover up his bouts with alcohol addiction. His constant drinking has cost him one job after another until he has reached the place where he no longer attempts to hold down a job. Work, for him, is a means of getting a few dollars for beverage alcohol and room rent, and finally just for beverage alcohol. Since his mind is so befuddled, he can't be used for work requiring skill.

His health is about gone, too. The body God gave him has finally begun to break down under constant neglect and abuse. Anyone who has ever visited skid row has seen evidences of the deterioration that grips these victims in the final stages of alcoholism. They stumble haltingly along the street like men twice their age. Walking is torture for them, and their hands tremble.

They eke out a miserable existence on handouts. Malnutrition is common. So are cirrhosis of the liver and nervous and gastric disorders. In France, where the incidence of alcoholism is higher than anywhere else in the world, the incidence of liver ailments is the highest.

I can speak personally about the gastric disorders that alcoholism causes. Because I burned my stomach up with beverage alcohol during my drinking days, I have stomach ulcers and assorted other digestive problems.

The alcoholic may have circulatory problems and break out in "wine sores," as we call them at the Mission. At this stage he is no stranger to hospitals. He has undoubtedly had the experience of collapsing and being taken to the charity ward in a hospital, where they have treated him as best they could. The medical profession finds working with such men or women a frustrating task. Their bodies have been abused so terribly they do not respond well to treatment. And, when they are discharged, they almost invariably go back to the bottle and continue the process of destroying themselves.

Even more disturbing than an alcoholic's physical deterioration is the way in which his mind deteriorates under the continual abuse of beverage alcohol. Every mission superintendent sees this effect of alcohol, even in former bankers, lawyers, investment brokers, business executives, and others who come in off the street.

The mind and personality of a former medical doctor, who finally died at a state institution, was so affected by his continual bouts with beverage alcohol that he could not learn to live outside an institution. This man, who at one time had been a useful member of society and highly respected and loved in his community, could not even be used in a minor way as a male nurse at the institution where he spent the final years of his life. Why? Because of his mental deterioration.

A wealthy Kansas wheat farmer whose net worth was judged at close to a million dollars was so ruined by alcohol that ten years later his fortune was gone and he was living on skid row. And he was just barely doing well enough at his dishwashing job to keep from losing it.

Not long ago a young man came into the Mission who took pride in the fact that he had not gone as far down as some of the fellows we have described here.

"Listen, Buster," I told him, "don't get so smug about that. You're on the road. You aren't all the way down yet, but just wait awhile. You'll get there."

The possibility of going all the way down faces any individual from the third stage down, also many of the social and habitual drinkers who haven't been drinking beverage alcohol long enough to be addicts. Fortunately, however, the individual does not *have* to reach the place of organic deterioration before he can be set free from the bondage of drink. At any place along the downward path he can face himself and his situation and throw off the shackles of alcohol addiction.

The sooner the individual reaches this place and is helped, the less hold beverage alcohol will have on him, and the easier it will be for him to be freed. The man or woman in the final stage of alcoholism is not impossible to reach by any means, for nothing is impossible with God. But the problems involved in helping him are much more grave than if he had sought help earlier.

For example, we had a music professor from a large high school who had only been an alcoholic for a year and a half when he came to us for help. Working with him was much different than working with men who had been alcoholics for ten or fifteen years because he responded to treatment and to suggestion much faster.

Unfortunately, nothing can be done for the alcoholic until he wants to be reached. You may recognize all the symptoms and know what the fellow needs, but you can't get through to him unless he wants help. We have reached the place, through long and sometimes bitter experience, where we refuse to talk to a person who doesn't ask us for help.

A pastor came to me on one occasion and urged me to visit a family in which the husband was an alcoholic. I tried to explain that my visit would be fruitless unless the husband wanted to be helped. But when the wife pleaded with me to see him, I agreed to.

I spent half the morning getting acquainted with him and developing a measure of rapport because I wanted him to have confidence in me. When finally he began to open up, and we were engaged in a very friendly discussion about his problem and the fact that there was a solution to it, his wife stepped into the room. As she listened, she was irritated by something he said and she began to tear him apart right in front of me. That ended any hope I had of trying to reach him. It was a miserable, embarrassing situation, and I soon took my leave of them.

In this case the man wasn't ready for help and didn't want it, so he didn't come to me. So when I went to him at his home, we didn't have the privacy we should have had. Furthermore, I hadn't had an opportunity to get acquainted with his wife, so I didn't know what to expect from her. Consequently, when she tore into her husband the way she did, I was helpless. Of course, I do realize that she had probably reached the point where she could contain herself no longer. All the humiliation and heartaches of the past and her present fear just exploded. Nevertheless, I am sure that my visit was a hindrance and not the help we had hoped it would be.

The alcoholic must reach a crisis point in his life before he will be open to guidance and help. In the language of Mission personnel, he has to "hit bottom." Bottom can be different in each individual life.

One well-known attorney was a prealcoholic when he "hit bottom." A fastidious dresser, well-mannered, and dignified, he was just the opposite when he was intoxicated. His wife tried to tell him what a fool he made of himself when he had drunk too much, but he wouldn't believe it. So, at a cocktail party she had a friend come in with a movie camera and shoot a roll of film. When he was sober, they screened it for him.

He never took another drink.

Various surveys have estimated that only 3 to 12 percent of alcohol addicts ever get on skid row. The vast majority are living in their communities, protected by their families and occasionally by their business associates. They hide in their prisons of shame, fearful of facing life. They don't know which way to go. Most do not even want to admit to themselves that they have a problem. They must be jolted by something that shocks them enough to cause them to hit bottom and begin to look up for answers.

Perhaps the man hits bottom when he loses his job for the first time and sees his wife and children and himself without any visible means of support. Perhaps he hits bottom when the children recognize the problem and speak about it.

One woman came to my office in desperation after such an experience. She had come home with a six-pack of beer. Her twelve-year-old son fell to his knees and grabbed her around the legs and cried, "Oh, Mommy, Mommy, please don't drink that stuff! You know what it does to you!"

What he said caused her to hit bottom. She began to seek help.

Another woman came to me about her husband. "I have told that man a hundred times that I was going to leave him if he didn't stop drinking."

"Have you ever left him?" I asked her.

"No."

"Well, leave him this time."

When her husband came home and found her gone, he was so stunned he realized he had to have help. Up until this moment he had thought she was only kidding. He had never seen himself as having a drinking problem. Now he knew that everything he had in life that was worth having would be gone unless he faced up to this problem and got some answers. Consequently, he began to look for ways out of his difficulty.

We who counsel alcoholics have to look for this type of experience. How to help the alcohol addict come to that crisis area in his life where he will seek help is the subject of the second section of this book: "Five Ways to Help the Alcoholic."

4

COMPLETING THE CYCLE

As WE WORKED WITH ALCOHOL ADDICTS through the years, a number of things used to disturb us—things we could not understand. We could understand how men and women started drinking socially and progressed downward until they hit bottom and faced up to the fact that they had a drinking problem. We knew they had a sincere desire to quit drinking. We were aware, too, that when they really wanted to quit, they were in a condition to be helped.

Some of the individuals we saw go through the awful agony of withdrawal were men who had lost their jobs or had seen their businesses fail. The mortgages on their homes had been foreclosed, and their wives had filed for divorce. In some cases their children had been put in children's homes or placed with foster parents. These men wanted to stay sober more than anything else in the world so they could get their families back and once more have a place of respectability in the community. Yet they went back to drinking. Why did they fail? What were the warning signs? Could anything be done to help them break the vicious circle in which they found themselves?

For years such questions perplexed us. A man came to the Mission one night who was obviously in need of medical attention. We took him to the hospital. When we got him to the door of the psychiatric ward he had a seizure. It took several attendants to put him in bed and hold him down until the medication they gave him began to calm him.

He was put in a private room, where he spent the terrifying days of withdrawal, seeing strange, frightening, crawling things on the wall. At last, medication and hospital care and a period of sobriety cleared away the hallucinations. The man's mind began to function again and the doctors released him from the hospital.

He had a sincere desire not to drink any more. Had he been a millionaire and able to buy sobriety for the rest of his life, he would have done so, even if it were to cost him his entire fortune. He was an intelligent person with a good future ahead of him. Only one obstacle blocked his path. Beverage alcohol. I was sure that this man had plenty of reasons to stay sober if anyone did. Still, in a matter of months, he was once more hitting the bottle.

The same thing happened in my own life.

I don't know how many times I tried to overcome the problem. I don't know how many times I told myself, "It's going to be different from now on. I'm *not* going to take another drink." But I wasn't any stronger than the man to whom I just referred. I, too, went back to drinking, time and again.

In our years of working with alcoholics, we observed a pattern, a cycle: The alcoholic decides to quit drinking; he goes into a period of abstinence, and then returns to drinking.

We asked God for wisdom and understanding, claiming the promise found in James 1:5: "If any lack wisdom let him ask of God who giveth liberally and upbraideth not." In answer to our prayer, God gave the insight that helped us to piece the pattern together, and we used this insight in our interviews with men who professed a saving knowledge of Christ. We discovered that, almost invariably, they followed the same cycle.

The last test was on a group of forty-five men on our rehabilitation program. All had made so many decisions to quit drinking that they had long since lost count. They had all gone back, in agony, into the awful blackness of alcohol addiction after being so determined to put it behind them.

"Yes," they all said, without exception, "that's the way it happened."

In understanding the alcoholic, it will help to consider this cycle and how it operates.

Although the cycle follows the same general pattern each time it is repeated, the length of time varies widely. A cycle could take a single week, three weeks, that many months, or even a number of years. A medical doctor with whom we came in contact took ten years to complete the cycle, but complete it he did.

Similarly, the segments or compartments the cycle is divided into don't take the same amount of time in each case. The individual's makeup, the life he has previously lived, and his current environment—all have their effect on the pattern.

During the cycle you see in the alcoholic four characteristics: (1) the desire never to take another drink, (2) pride of sobriety, (3) fear of drinking again, and (4) the feeling that he has finally mastered the situation.

1. *The desire never to take another drink.*

The alcoholic has "had it." He's never going through this again. He's never going to be as sick as he was this time. Never again will he go through the terrible nightmare of an alcoholic blackout. Never again will he have to pick up the pieces again after an episode when he didn't even know for sure what he had done. Never again will he wake up in a strange town, not knowing when he got on or off the train. Never again does he want to go through the experience of being terribly shaken by the fact that he's in a place where he doesn't know anyone, that he doesn't have a single friend anywhere close to whom he can turn. Never again will he experience the feeling of guilt and remorse that flooded his heart as he finally began to sober up.

No, never again.

Just remembering the past keeps him sober for a time. Things go fairly well.

2. Pride of sobriety.

The alcoholic begins to take pride in the fact that he isn't drinking. For some time he hasn't had any tremors in his stomach. The cobwebs begin to leave his mind, and he's feeling more like himself again.

The Bible warns us not to think of ourselves more highly than we ought to think, also that we should take heed when we think we stand, lest we fall. Pride is dangerous.

Men often say to me, "You know, Jerry, I haven't had a drink in three weeks."

Someone else says, "I haven't had a drink in a month, and I want you to know that I'm proud of it. I'm so thankful that I don't take any of that stuff any more."

It isn't long until they have a superior attitude when they're watching the fellows around them who are still drinking. "Did you see the way that guy acted? I'd never do anything like that—and in front of such nice people."

These men have forgotten that they used to act the same way, and they begin to swell with pride because they think they have the situation under control. *They* don't drink any more!

Such thinking often coincides with the time the alcoholic starts to work again and is just beginning to produce. He has earned a little money, has bought himself some new clothes, and is beginning to enjoy the feel of having a few dollars in his pocket. He has returned to his home and his wife and children. His children are beginning to trust him once more, and his wife is beginning to treat him like a human being. Things are going along just fine. He's never been happier. The first thing he does when he sees you is tell you about the progress he has made and that he's getting back to the old feel of things. Pride of attainment shows in his facial expressions, his speech, and actions. But something is gnawing at him. Something he probably doesn't mention to anyone.

3. *The fear of drinking again.*

Even though he longs to remain an abstainer, he has the urge to drink. In understanding that, one must not forget that this individual is trying to make a comeback in a society where, according to some estimates, 70 percent of the adult males and 58 percent of the adult females drink. Social drinking is the accepted thing.

He feels that he has to have a little social life, and common sense tells him that he's got to go to company parties, sales meetings, and that sort of thing in connection with his job. Yet, in the circles he travels in, it is difficult to go anywhere without having someone offer him a drink.

He's still very proud of his attainment. He's as proud as ever over the fact that he doesn't drink. He can still remember what it was like when he was hitting the bottle heavily. He realizes that there is a chance he might lose all he has gained through his comeback on the road to sobriety and respectability. The fear that he is going to take another drink begins to build.

This is the area we call a "dry drunk." This man has reached the place where he has to fight against taking another drink. He is disgusted with people who drink. He can't stand the smell of liquor. He becomes irritable, and even someone's suggestion that he take a drink becomes a personal insult.

At the same time he begins to fight every beer sign that's hanging along the street, every ad he sees in the newspaper or on television for alcoholic beverages. Of all men, he is the most miserable while he wages a continual fight to keep from drinking and keep his hold on the life he now has.

A short time ago I received a terse note from a business executive who wrote, "Jerry, this is still no picnic. Thanks to you, I do know the scrap I have on my hands. I surely hope the Lord intends for me to make the grade." There is a tone of hopelessness in his letter, a feeling that he is alone in his desperate battle to keep from taking another drink.

It would be easy to pity the man at this point, but pity is another thing that can be devastating to the alcoholic's chances of attaining release. Pity can weaken his determination to fight the urge to drink and bring him to the conclusion that it's no use to try to remain sober.

The pressure against the individual who is fighting alcohol addiction is tremendous. Society encourages him to drink. It does so with a social life where the person who does not drink is looked upon as an oddball. It does so through advertising media—newspapers, magazines, billboards, radio, and TV. It does so through movies and television stories where beverage alcohol is freely consumed.

At the same time society condemns the man if he lets his consumption of liquor get out of control. Just as pity is a definite hindrance to helping the alcoholic, so is condemnation.

Neither pity nor condemnation provides help. Only by better understanding the person who is addicted to alcohol can we hope to help him.

As the fight to keep from drinking increases in intensity, something else is happening. Since the individual has not been drinking, his mind is becoming clearer. He can think better, and the physical effects of his excessive drinking are beginning to disappear. He is feeling more and more like the normal, respectable person he used to be.

Combined with the pride that he hasn't taken a drink for quite a while is the feeling that he has reached the place where he's finally going to be able to manage his life again. He's really a different person than he was when he had his drinking problems.

Another factor that affects the alcoholic is the philosophy that the alcoholic is a person with some sort of a mental problem, a personality quirk, or some type of neurosis that has caused him to be like he is. Or, so the theory goes, he has had some physiological problem that has caused him to drink to excess.

Dr. Clyde Narramore, in his pamphlet *Alcoholism,* suggests several possible causes for alcoholism. The individual may be trying to hide from life. He may have reverted to alcoholism because of the pressures and disturbances of the day. Dr. Narramore says that the chronic alcoholic is emotionally maladjusted and in most cases was maladjusted before he became addicted to alcohol.

He calls attention to some physiological reasons for alcohol addiction: "For example, the possibility of becoming an alcoholic is greater in persons who have undergone a condition known as anoxia at birth. This means that there was insufficient oxygen available for the body tissues. Also, it is known that certain neurological impairments can increase the probability of an individual becoming captured by drink. A complete physical examination should always be made while determining the cause of an alcoholic condition."*

A pastor friend of mine was counseling with a man who had graduated from Bible school. As a young man he felt called to the ministry. He had an opportunity to get a good

*Psychology for Living Series, No. 6, *Alcoholism,* by Dr. Clyde M. Narramore, p. 5.

sales franchise when he was still a student working part time. When he got out of school he decided to work for a couple of years to make a little money before taking a pastorate. He got more deeply involved in making money and, forgetting God's call, he began to grow cold spiritually. He took his first drink with a customer. It wasn't long until he was hopelessly addicted to alcohol. He lost his business, and his family was soon much hungrier than they ever would have been as a poor preacher's family.

The alcoholic who is struggling to make a recovery and is fighting his burning desire to drink may also have some psychological, physical or spiritual problem to add considerably to his difficulties.

As he is beginning to recover, he is also saying to himself, "I'm feeling better physically and mentally than I've ever felt in my life. I feel great."

Somehow he feels that he has overcome the problems that caused him to drink or have greatly aggravated his situation. He may feel that he's all right spiritually because he has started going to church again, even though he has never had a personal experience with Christ.

In spite of the battle he is having with his old desires to drink, he begins to feel good. Because of that he thinks that everything is finally all right.

He moves on.

4. *The feeling that he has finally mastered the situation.*

He begins to think that he can handle this thing. At last he's got it under control.

The Scriptures warn us that pride always goes before a fall. Peter was so sure that he would die with Christ rather than deny Him. But later, when he was asked if he also was a follower of Christ, he cursed and said he didn't even know Him. The alcoholic who is so sure he has finally mastered his problem is like Peter in his self-confidence.

It must be remembered that the alcoholic is still in the world of social drinking. Ever since he first started to make a comeback, he has been pressured to drink by people who can't stand to see someone who has more courage and willpower and good judgment than themselves.

Such people used to throw their taunts at me. I know just what it's like. "Aw, you can handle it. What's the matter with you? Are you a man or a mouse? You know you'll be able to handle this little drink."

Just saying no doesn't stop their efforts to persuade him to drink. They continue their pressure to make him take a drink. "You know you'll be able to handle this one little drink. Now, come on, have one with me for old time's sake."

Ever since he came off that last, terrible drunk he has been refusing such offers. At first, he turned them down because he actually didn't want a drink. He was too close to his last drunk and didn't want to risk another one.

A little later he still says no, but his reason for doing so has changed. For a time he didn't drink because he was proud that he didn't. He looked down on those who tried to urge it on him. Now he doesn't drink because he's fighting it. He's scared to death that he's going to break down at some time and will be in trouble again. (All of this is so subtle he may not realize it unless he stops short and examines his motives.)

Then comes the final step.

Things have been going so well for him he has become complacent about his problem of alcohol addiction. He has been given more responsibility at work. His wife is trusting him more than she has for some time. His children have more confidence in him and that increases his confidence in himself. He's the master of a whole new world. He is now back to the place where he was when he first started to drink socially—or so he thinks. When he is urged to take a drink, he does so, thinking that by now he surely ought to be able to handle it.

What happens after that doesn't follow a set pattern. If he has taken one drink and was able to stop before he got drunk, he feels more proud of himself than ever because he thinks he can again drink socially and handle it. His guard goes down, and he loses a bit of his fear of beverage alcohol.

Or one drink might set the fires of alcoholism to raging out of control in his life. One drink can create an insatiable thirst that will not be quenched. One drink might be enough to plunge him to the very depths of alcoholism as quickly as one can be pushed over a cliff.

The alcoholic who takes another drink—whether he takes the slow route or the fast route—will experience the same end result: He will once again be completely and totally victimized by alcohol addiction.

For example, I was working with a fellow who had me stumped. I knew him very well and couldn't figure out what was building the fire in him that caused him to turn back to the bottle. Everything seemed to be going along fine. His wife was a lovely Christian person and he had been taken in by her friends and their husbands in a fine way, so he wasn't with people who would encourage him to drink. Yet, he had started to drink again. I couldn't understand why.

Then one day when I was talking with his wife she said, "You know, my husband drinks near beer. He just likes the taste of beer and, since it doesn't have any alcohol in it, he's been drinking it."

"There!" I exclaimed. "That's what has been causing the trouble."

Although there isn't much ethyl alcohol in near beer there is a little—$\frac{1}{2}$ of 1 percent. That doesn't sound like much, does it? It isn't. But for some reason, the trace of ethyl alcohol in the near beer he drank was enough to start him to drinking again. He had reached the same place in alcoholism that diabetics reach when they have no tolerance for sugar. Ethyl alcohol triggers such a fierce thirst and craving in the alcoholic that he goes back into drunkenness once more.

Earlier in this chapter we mentioned a doctor who had a ten-year cycle. By drinking half a glass of beer, he started on another drunk that brought him to the ruination of his home and cost him his practice. Previously an alcoholic, he had fought his way up through the cycle. He had won back his practice and was building a very good life for himself.

His friends drank, however, and since he felt he should serve them liquor when he entertained them in his apartment, he kept a supply of liquor on hand. For some reason that is difficult to understand, people who are drinking don't feel at ease if someone in the crowd abstains from drinking. In order to make his guests feel comfortable, he would pour half a glass of beer and set it in front of him, never touching it.

He married a second time and went out to San Francisco for a reunion of his old navy buddies, taking his bride along. As usual, he poured half a glass of beer and set it in front of him. While everybody was spinning yarns about the old days, he reached out and drank the half glass of beer. At the Mission much later, he told us that he had downed it before he even realized what he was doing.

Although he was a highly intelligent individual that half glass of beer was enough to pull the trigger. Eventually Doc ended up on skid row.

There is a period in the cycle of chronic alcoholism in which the individual's body once more begins to deteriorate. The same situations happen to him, the same DT's terrify him, the same despair grips his soul like an ugly recurring nightmare until the fellow once more reaches the place where he can't take it any longer. He never wants to have another drink.

He has come full circle back to the place he started from. And, unhappily, the cycle will repeat and keep repeating until some way is found to break it.

When the alcoholic is at the bottom and has come to the place where he doesn't want to take another drink, then we can help him to break the cycle. The cycle can be broken. We can thank God for that. He has provided a way of escape. This will be developed much more fully in the second section of the book, but we will consider it briefly here.

1. *Encourage him in his desire to stop.*
2. *Help him to face his problem.*
3. *Provide him with medical care, so that he can have the help modern medicine can give him. See that he gets a complete physical checkup.*
4. *Help him to understand that he can't overcome alcohol addiction by himself.*
5. *Introduce him to the power of God.*
6. *Teach him to keep in daily touch with God's power.*

This is the way we will be able to help the alcoholic to break the cycle and overcome addiction. It is possible for him to be completely free from the power of alcohol addiction.

This is what we must aim for and encourage the alcoholic to strive for. It isn't enough to be satisfied with just being sober. He should come to that place where he has real victory in every phase of his life through faith in the Lord Jesus Christ. This faith will give him victory over this drinking *now*, and will give him a place with God in all eternity. This needs to be our goal in our aim for the successful treatment of the alcoholic.

One thing that impresses me a great deal at the Mission, whether it is in talking with one of the men from the street or an "up and out" alcoholic, is that every case is different.

The approach to the problem is different with every individual because God hasn't made us all the same.

For that reason there is no standard procedure; there are no hard and fast rules that can be followed in every case. Yet I am always conscious of the fact that God is always vitally interested in every man who comes. God is willing to give us the wisdom and insight needed in every case, if we will only look to Him and not to man for our answer.

That does not mean we should not use psychiatrists or doctors or sociologists. God gave us men in those professions to help with this and other problems. But we must not lose sight of the fact that in the last analysis God is the One who heals. He is the One who must heal the alcoholic of his addiction and restore him to a place of respectability in his community, but, of course, with his cooperation.

5

HINDRANCES TO RECOVERY

DR. STEPHEN A. SEYMOUR, who operates the Stephen A. Seymour Hospital for Alcoholics in Los Angeles, California, also writes a column for the *Wilshire Press* on the subject. In one of his columns he was asked this question.

DEAR DOCTOR:

What gives you the greatest problem in the treatment of difficult case histories? Is it delirium tremens, malnutrition, vitamin deficiency or temporary insanity?

JOAN H.

Dr. Seymour replied:

DEAR JOAN H.:

The biggest problem is in treating the members of the patient's family who don't drink.

How true this is!

At the Mission we have found one of our greatest problems in helping a man back to usefulness is his family.

For varying lengths of time the alcoholic has hurt everyone around him. This is particularly true of those who love him the most. He has lied to them, abused them, and made them suffer in a way that few who have not been close to such an individual can possibly understand.

The hurt the alcoholic brings to his family is not necessarily intentional on his part. In his progression down into alcoholism he has experienced a complete breakdown of his personality. Whatever he has been before, he is now a selfish, self-centered person. He has a burning desire for beverage alcohol and wants to destroy anything that stands in the way of his securing it. Often, as he sees it, his family is the chief obstacle in his way.

From personal experience I know this to be true. My heart still aches as I remember sitting in my living room and looking at my own family (my wife and three children) with a strange, unnatural loathing. I had a good job. I was respected in the community. Yet the craving for drink burned so fiercely within me that it was the only thing that mattered. It meant more than family or job or friends.

They weren't going to stand in my way any longer, I reasoned. They didn't need to think that they could hold me down. I was going to leave; that was what I was going to do. They weren't going to keep me from drinking.

My wife and family had never given me any reason to feel as I did. They hadn't nagged at me or tried to interfere with my life. Their only fault was that they were there, standing between me and my beloved bottle. I just couldn't take it.

So I left home and went on a two-year drunk that lasted until I was brought up short by a drastic situation that stopped me from drinking.

Leaving my family was a despicable thing to do, but at the time my thinking was so warped that it seemed very logical and natural. According to my way of looking at the situation, *I* was the one who had been abused. *I* was the one who felt injured and hurt. *I* was the one who had been put upon so terribly that I could not longer take it. So I had rebelled. I didn't see how anyone could blame me for what I'd done.

During that period I didn't give much thought to what my

actions had done to my family. Our oldest son had been hurt and grew resentful because of the way I had treated his mother and his younger brother and sister. Our daughter was bewildered at having her father leave, and, because her mother had to work to support the family, was placed in an orphanage. Our littlest guy was too young to understand what was happening but could sense the confusion and unhappiness that swirled about him and blighted his young life.

My wife loved me, and she had stayed by me through everything that had happened, yet I deserted her. She was forced to earn the living for herself and the children and had to assume the role of both mother and father. Our entire family was bruised and hurt by my actions.

When I finally came back home, although I had found Christ as my Saviour and was determined to live for Him, they had a terrific adjustment to make. It wasn't easy for them to accept the fact that I had returned and wanted to make amends for the hurt and grief I had caused them. It was hard for them to believe that I wouldn't do the same thing again.

I don't think I realized the full extent of what I had done and how it had affected my family until some years later, when my wife and I went to visit our oldest son and his family. One morning he bared his heart to me, as he and I were out for a drive. "Your prayers must be paying off, Dad," he said suddenly. "I quit hating your guts three months ago."

Most of the time he had been very nice to me, but deep within him the hurt lay—an ugly, open wound. He loved me. I'm sure of that. He just couldn't stand the thought of being hurt so deeply again. For that reason he withheld himself from me.

My wife's reaction was different. Although she had drifted far from God, she knew Christ as her Saviour. She realized that God was still sovereign and that somehow He would work things out. She had some serious adjustments to make, but through God's love in her heart she was able to overcome the terrible hurt and accept me into our home once more.

Our two younger children had little difficulty in accepting me. They saw me in the newness of the life of Christ, and His love warmed their hearts and took away their hurt.

Although we had problems and difficulties in making the adjustments necessary in a life together, some of the families we have tried to help have had considerably more trouble than we did.

Often the inclination of the alcoholic's family is either to pity him for the plight he finds himself in or to swing to the opposite extreme and reject him. Neither course will do him any good. What he needs is intelligent understanding.

A wife will often become oversympathetic when she is trying to win her husband away from beverage alcohol. Because of that she will do things that will actually be a hindrance and a stumbling block to him.

Take the distraught woman who called me one holiday season. Her husband had been drinking and was involved in an automobile accident. No one had been hurt, but because he was drunk when the accident happened, he was jailed. She wanted me to see if I could do anything to help him get out of jail.

I had had some contact with her husband before. He was concerned about his drinking and was looking for help. Thinking that this might be the time when I could help him spiritually I made arrangements with a bondsman and met the wife at the city jail. Bond was set, and he was released.

The next thing I knew, the man had lost his job and was on a real drunk. I couldn't understand it.

But that wasn't the end of my contacts with him. Some time later I was called back into the case when things were in a worse mess than before. The family was out of money and hungry. The husband was in that terrible, bitter, accusing state alcoholics so often get into when they hate everybody and everything that stands in the way of their drinking. When I arrived at their home, I asked him, "How in the world did you get in this state? You had time when you were in jail to get the liquor out of your system, and you had a chance to go back to work the next day. What started you on this binge?"

He didn't answer, but his wife did, and her answer stunned me.

"I knew he'd be so shaky and feel so terrible after being in jail and being taken off liquor so suddenly," she said, "so on the way home I stopped and got him a six-pack of beer and a pint of whisky."

I didn't say a word. I couldn't. I got up and left.

Another woman wanted her husband to go to AA. He said to her, "I'll make a bargain with you. I'll go to AA if you'll give me a half pint of whisky every time I go."

She was so anxious for him to start attending the AA meetings that she entered into the agreement. After he had attended a number of their meetings, she realized he wasn't being helped. The half pint of whisky she was giving him each time he attended was spoiling anything the organization could do for him and was keeping him drunk and separated from a normal life with his family.

Regardless of how well-meaning a person is, such sympathy for the alcoholic can only hinder any attempt he makes to quit drinking.

Bitterness and rejection can be just as bad as pity.

Although the wife and family of every alcoholic suffer unspeakably, they must forgive and forget if they want to see this husband and father restored as a respected member of their family and of society.

Forgiving is never easy. And it is particularly hard when

the wife runs the risk of being hurt again. It is so difficult, in fact, that only by a complete surrender to Christ can a wife take her erring husband back and accept him without reservation.

There are other ways in which the wife of an alcoholic can be a hindrance. Not long ago, one of the churches brought to our attention a family in which there were eight children. The father was an alcoholic. Often there wasn't food in the house for them to eat. The church was able to provide food and help in a material way, but they asked us to aid in the rehabilitation of the father.

From time to time the man stopped drinking during the period we were counseling him, but he always went back to it again.

It was difficult to understand just why he went back to drinking again and again. He was a very fine musician, I learned, and had played and sung with country-music bands from one coast to the other. He would probably have stayed with this vocation had he not had such a large family. They were one hindrance.

"I'd like to go back," he would tell me wistfully. He spoke of it so often I began to see that one of the factors in his drinking problem was his feeling that he had failed his family by not getting back with a band where he could earn enough money to support his children. That was a second hindrance.

Then one day I learned something else that made the picture more clear. I was visiting him one afternoon when I noticed that his wife wasn't there.

"She's at work."

"Oh, is she working now?" I asked.

"Yes, she's working and I'm baby-sitting," he blurted out miserably. The words rushed out. "I'd like to get a job, but she doesn't want me to. She wants me to baby-sit so she can work." His eyes met mine. "And that's not being a man. I've *got* to be a man!"

But his wife had seen the time when her children had gone hungry because he had failed them. Now she had an opportunity to work and she took it. She *knew* that she would stay on the job. Her normal mother instinct of wanting to provide for her children was also destroying what she wanted most out of life—a husband and father who would provide for her and her children.

Some of the case histories from our files at the Mission provide an insight into some of the underlying reasons why some men cannot quit drinking.

One man wrote, "I'm not trying to blame anyone. I only want to show what could be one of the reasons for my excessive drinking. In twenty-five years of marriage my wife never once told me she loved me. . . . By nature I'm a very affectionate person, and I constantly showed my love toward my wife and daughter, but my wife never returned any of my love. After we were separated for four years she told me that her mind controlled her emotions."

For lack of love this fellow began to do more and more drinking until he was drinking excessively. Consequently he turned into a chronic alcoholic.

The inability of one's life partner to return the affection of the other will turn women as well as men to drinking and alcoholism.

Another underlying cause for a man's turning to drink is lack of cleanliness in the home. This is an area of real difficulty for the counselor who is trying to help the family make the adjustments that will help to return the alcoholic husband to sobriety. The very fact that the wife is a poor housekeeper presents a serious problem. The house is always dirty and cluttered, the kids' faces need scrubbing and their clothes need washing and mending.

It may be that the wife is overworked and run-down, or so distraught she has let the housework slide. It may be that she has never learned to keep house, or that she simply isn't ambitious enough to clean it up and keep it clean. But, whatever the reason, the dirt and physical confusion of the home can add to the mental confusion of the alcoholic and make it more difficult for him to keep off beverage alcohol.

Let's take a look at the situation from the alcoholic's point of view. He knows that he has messed up his life, but he's more anxious than ever to get his family back. Now that he's put the bottle aside, he is going to clean up his life. He comes back home eager for things to be different.

But when he gets there, home isn't any different than it used to be. The sink is stacked with dirty dishes, and the stove hasn't been cleaned for a year. Newspapers are strewn all over the floor, covering the pans the baby was playing with two days before. Under the bed is dirt that was there six months ago, and the odor of dirty diapers drifts in from the bathroom. It's the same dirty old hole he used to live in. His wife's habits haven't changed a bit. He was foolish to think he could change.

I don't exactly understand why a dirty house should be a hindrance to a man who's trying to shake alcohol addiction. But it is. To have success with an alcoholic who is married to a poor housekeeper, the counselor must make her see the importance of a clean, attractive home.

Just as some wives are careless about their home and the care of the children, some husbands are careless about their finances. This can cause a very serious problem for the wife who drinks socially.

If the husband is irresponsible in caring for the needs of his family and is extravagant and irresponsible in the way he handles his financial affairs, bill collectors start hounding this husband and wife, and the bank calls, telling them their checking account is overdrawn. The wife is humiliated, angry, and worried. If she is a social drinker, she may begin to drink more to hide from her problems, and it will be only a matter of time until she becomes an alcoholic.

If such a woman is to be helped, her husband must be helped to handle his financial matters in such a way as to remove the pressures that have been causing his wife to drink.

Another hindrance is the guilt complex that enshrouds the family of the alcoholic man or woman. The nondrinking or social-drinking members of the family who are not yet addicted to alcohol are terribly ashamed. They are ashamed of the way the alcoholic has acted in the neighborhood or in front of guests in the home. They find it difficult to accept the fact that their loved one is addicted. Their shame is often so great that they will not seek outside help until the situation is so serious they must.

Not long ago a businessman called me in desperation and wanted to know what could be done about his wife. "She's an alcoholic," he said. "I finally had to do something with her so I put her in the hospital, but she's just as bad off now as she was when she went in."

The rest of his story was just as discouraging. The doctors recommended that she be sent to a sanitorium for a year, and that would cost about $18,000. "I can afford that for a little while," he said miserably, "but not for long."

This couple belonged to the country club set. Among their friends drinking was the accepted method of entertaining. Both of them drank socially, but the wife was more susceptible to alcohol than her husband was. She became involved in cocktail parties, the programming, and bridge clubs, where she consumed more and more liquor. Her desire to be popular, to be well thought of by people who mattered, and to be included in the activities of society became a stumbling block and sent her into alcoholism. Now she was to be hospitalized for a year at great expense.

Social drinking, itself, presents a problem when one is trying to get the alcoholic to a place where he can make a proper adjustment with his family.

I have a friend who has been sober for more than sixteen years. The other day he told me that his wife is going back to a little social drinking. "She likes a glass of beer on a warm summer day," he explained. "I can't see anything much wrong with that, so I buy it for her."

He doesn't realize what a dangerous spot he is in. The alcoholic cycle we explained in chapter 4 shows why.

The very fact that his wife is drinking can set this man fighting to keep from drinking, and throw him into the dry drunk stage. He sees her enjoying a drink. There is more in the refrigerator. All he has to do is go out and take one. One of these days he might become tired of fighting his desire for a glass of beer and, unless he has given himself over to the Lord completely, he may not be strong enough spiritually to resist. The first time he opens a can of beer and drinks it, he will be in big trouble.

A similar and perhaps even more serious problem exists for alcoholic women whose husbands drink socially. He has liquor in the house, although it is understood that his wife is not to drink.

What he forgets is that when he leaves for work, she remains home for from eight to sixteen hours a day. Here is this poor woman whose thirst all but consumes her at times—with liquor readily available all of that time, and much of the day there is no one with her to persuade her not to drink. I suppose it would be possible for a woman alcoholic to make a comeback under circumstances like that, but it would be very, very difficult.

Although there are many hindrances in family relationships to cause difficulty for the alcoholic who is struggling to rehabilitate himself, he can overcome any of them through a right relationship with God and a good solid grounding in the Christian faith. It is imperative that we aim for these in the alcoholic's life.

6

WHAT GOD SAYS

EVERY NOW AND THEN a fellow comes staggering into my office at the Mission, shakes a drunken finger in my face, and slurs a challenge at me.

"Jerry," he says, his voice mushing the words, "it's all right for me to drink. The Bible says that it's all right for me to drink! I dare you to show me any place in the Bible where it says that I can't drink!"

Or, as happened one time, a woman who is obviously in her cups will call on the telephone. "I know I drink," she announced defiantly, "but I've been saved and I know I'm saved. If I was so stin¹.in' drunk I fell in the gutter an' died, I *know* that I'd go to Heaven!"

What do you say to people like that? And what scriptural basis do you have for what you say?

For a long while this was a big problem to me. Back in 1948 when I accepted the Lord Jesus Christ as my Saviour I simply took Him at His Word. Some of the Scripture verses I rested on were: "For whosoever shall call upon the name of the Lord shall be saved" (Romans 10:13).

"He that heareth my word, and believeth on him that sent me, hath everlasting life, and shall not come into condemnation; but is passed from death unto life" (John 5:24).

"But as many as received him, to them gave he power to

become the sons of God, even to them that believe on his name" (John 1:12).

"For by grace are ye saved through faith; and that not of yourselves: it is the gift of God: Not of works, lest any man should boast" (Ephesians 2:8-9).

"So then faith cometh by hearing, and hearing by the word of God" (Romans 10:17).

I was convinced in my heart and mind of the truth of the Scriptures, and I had found Christ as my Saviour. I knew that I had been given a new life, for the Bible said so: "Therefore if any man be in Christ, he is a new creature: old things are passed away; behold, all things are become new" (II Corinthians 5:17).

Then I began to hear temperance lectures in which the speakers went to great lengths to explain that there were two Hebrew words, *yayin* and *tirosh,* and two Greek words, *oinos* and *gleukos,* which were translated as "wine" in English. Yet, so the speakers declared, one word in each language meant unfermented wine and the other referred to fermented wine.

I searched the Scriptures and read what authorities had to say on the subject but could find no place where the statements concerning different meanings of the two words were borne out. Dr. Roland H. Bainton, professor of Ecclesiastical History at Yale University, wrote in *Christianity Today**** that all four words refer to fermented wine, and he quotes the portions of Scripture that prove it.

The interpretation of the temperance people bothered me a great deal. I believe the Bible is the Word of God. I believe it says what it means and means what it says, and that it needs no other interpreter. I based my salvation upon it—my hope for Eternal life.

***Roland H. Bainton, "Total Abstinence and Biblical Principles," *Christianity Today, II* (July 7, 1958), 23.

When I tell a man that he is born again and has new life because the Word of God says so, I believe it with all my heart. I believe that he can trust the promises of God and can take the Bible for just exactly what it says.

Take this person who is trying to trap me into an argument. Suppose I try to explain away the word "wine" in the Bible. Suppose I tell him that it doesn't really mean wine, even though it says wine. Then I talk with him later that day or the next morning when he is starting to sober up. I tell him the same thing I told him before and then take him into the Book of Romans. I quote Romans 10:9-10: "That if thou shalt confess with thy mouth the Lord Jesus, and shalt believe in thine heart that God hath raised him from the dead, thou shalt be saved. For with the heart man believeth unto righteousness; and with the mouth confession is made unto salvation."

He makes a decision for Christ, and when we have finished praying, I say, "Now, you can know that you are saved."

He turns this over in his mind, and then asks, "How can I know that?"

"The Word of God says so."

"Now wait a minute!" The danger signals go up. Questions flame in his eyes. "When I was talking to you about wine you said the Bible doesn't really mean wine. Now you say the Bible says that I'm saved. How can I believe you? Maybe it means something else when it says that I'm saved."

This is a hypothetical case, of course. But with the type of men I was working with, that is just exactly what would have happened. And I couldn't have used any argument that wasn't scriptural. In searching the Scriptures, I wasn't able to find anything the Bible said against drinking, but the Bible does have a lot to say against drunkenness. One of the familiar ones is Proverbs 20:1: "Wine is a mocker, strong drink is raging: and whosoever is deceived thereby is not wise."*

The Bible does not say anything about not drinking wine, except to several different classes of people. When wine was used in the prescribed way according to God's plan and purpose, He accepted it. But when man's misuse of wine resulted in drunkenness, God condemned this drunkenness.

So, when a person challenges me to show him in the Bible where it says he shouldn't drink (and this happens very often) I have an answer. I say, "Friend of mine, the Bible doesn't say that you shouldn't drink."

He usually blinks his eyes at that.

And I go on, "There isn't any place in the Bible where it says that you shouldn't drink. But it does have a lot to say about getting drunk. Let me give you a few examples." And then I read some Bible verses along this line. Then I proceed to show him in the Word that he is a sinner, that he needs a Saviour because he has committed a sin against the Holy God by getting drunk.

He has been thrown off guard. Instead of an argument, which is what he expected, he has been brought face to face with his sin and the provision God has made through Christ to forgive him and make him a new man, if only he will trust in Christ.

Read Jeremiah 13:9-14 and you will find that God uses beverage alcohol as a judgment. And again, later in the same book, you read: *"Make ye him drunken; for he magnified himself against the Lord: Moab also shall wallow in his vomit, and he also shall be in derision"* (Jeremiah 48:26).

By reading the Scriptures we see that there are a number of things that go hand in hand with drunkenness: immorality,

*Additional references are: Proverbs 23:29-35; Isaiah 5:11-14, 5:22-23; Isaiah 28:3, 28:7, 56:9-12; Hosea 3:1, 4:11, 7:5; Amos 2:8; Eph. 5:18; Gal. 5:21. The WCTU publishes 75 Bible verses on excessive drinking. There are 627 such verses in the Bible.

rebellion against God, the destruction of man. Is it any wonder that God hates drunkenness and puts a curse upon the drunkard?

The more carefully I study the subject in the Bible, the stronger is my conviction that it is basically the product and not the individual which causes alcoholism. Read Jeremiah 13:13 again, and you will note the prophecy says that God is going to use drunkenness to bring destruction to the nation. He did not say that He was going to make all people psychoneurotic and this would be the reason wine would get them in its clutches.

It is interesting to note that history reveals that sixteen civilizations have fallen because of drunkenness. When we see the tragic increase in alcoholism in America today we cannot but wonder whether God is going to use this means of bringing judgment against our great nation for turning against Him.

As an alcoholic myself I know what would happen to me personally if I took another drink. Of course, that is one of the reasons I practice abstinence.

But that is not the reason we believe in total abstinence for Christians.

A good case against using any beverage alcohol can be made just by examining the results of drinking, but these facts are not necessarily enough. For example:

I could take you down to any rescue mission and let you observe what beverage alcohol has done to men's minds and bodies. I could show you the squalid little skid row mortuary just off Madison Street in Chicago where funerals are held every day for the victims of alcohol who have died on the street or in cheap flophouses. They are buried from the dirty, storefront parlor without a single mourner at their ten-minute services. Usually a man from the nearby rescue mission is there to say a word and offer prayer, but that is all.

We could go to the case history files of almost any mission and find grim, painful stories of the way alcohol destroys dignity and personal integrity. We have the accounts of men who confessed to stealing the groceries their wives have bought (probably with the last money in the house) to feed their families; the accounts of men who stole the very shoes off their children's feet and sold them to get money enough for a bottle of cheap wine.

I know from personal experience the agony and terror of delirium tremens, when the bed seems to shake so violently the alcoholic is afraid he will fall out of it; when he dozes off into a half stupor—half asleep, only to be awakened to see that the entire room is covered with weird, writhing, crawling things; when he is so terrified he screams against them and thinks he will die of fright.

But, for some reason, referring to such cases is not very effective in keeping a young person from beverage alcohol, or in getting a social drinker to stop. A mixture of pride and personal superiority makes the average individual think, "Oh, I know stuff like that happens to people who are so weak they cannot control themselves or their liquor. But I'm not made that way. I'm strong. I'll be able to drink what I want to and keep from taking too much."

Temperance has long been taught in the schools. Not long ago, a survey made by the state of Kansas on the effect of such temperance teaching revealed some interesting facts. According to the questionnaires filled out by high school youngsters across Kansas, the schools' efforts to promote temperance meant very little.

They were asked, "Where do you think the teaching of temperance is effective?"

The overwhelming majority replied that the temperance teaching they received in their church was the most effective.

This means that we, as Christians, have both the greatest opportunity and the greatest responsibility in the matter.

Our teaching of abstinence can be most effective if we base it solidly upon a personal relationship to the Lord Jesus Christ. For, although I have to tell the drunks who challenge me that there is no place in the Bible that says they shouldn't drink, there is strong scriptural basis for total abstinence for the Christian.

A study of drinking in the Word of God leads one to the discovery that there were two classes of people who were told they should not drink. Priests and kings were ordered to abstain from beverage alcohol for a specific reason. (See Leviticus 10:8-11; Proverbs 31:4-5.)

Priests were ordered not to drink during their course in the Temple so they could tell the difference between the holy and the unholy and could teach the people the difference between the good and the bad.

Kings and princes were not to drink for the same reason. They were to abstain from drink so they could tell the difference between right and wrong and be fair in their judgment of the people who came before them.

As we consider what the Bible says, we should not forget that the Old Testament is very clear in its admonition to priests and kings to abstain from beverage alcohol.

The Book of Revelation states that those who have accepted Christ as Saviour are kings and priests:

"And from Jesus Christ, the faithful *and* trustworthy Witness, the First-born of the dead [that is, first to be brought back to life] and the Prince (Ruler) of the kings of the earth. To Him Who ever loves us and has once [for all] loosed *and* freed us from our sins by His own blood, . . . And formed us into a kingdom [a royal race] priests to His God and Father, to Him be the glory and the power *and* the majesty and the dominion throughout the ages *and* forever and ever. Amen, so be it" (Revelation 1:5-6, The Amplified New Testament).

The Apostle Peter also says that we became kings and priests. We are members of a royal family. "But ye are a chosen generation, a royal priesthood, an holy nation, a peculiar people" (I Peter 2:9).

Because of our salvation through faith in Christ we have become sons, the adopted sons of the King. As such we are members of the King's family and the orders that went out to the kings and priests apply to us. We are not to drink so that we will have clear judgment and discernment as God's representatives in this world.

"As the Father hath sent me, so send I you," Jesus told His disciples. As Christians we are sent to witness, to teach the people. This is the responsibility of the believer. "Go ye therefore [into all the world], and teach . . .," the Lord Jesus Christ instructed His disciples. In order to teach, we must know the difference between right and wrong.

Therefore I believe we as believers are not to drink beverage alcohol.

On one occasion after I presented this thesis to a youth group a young man got to his feet and said, "The Bible says that the priest isn't supposed to drink when he's in the temple, but what about when he's outside the temple? It doesn't mention that."

"That's true," I told him. "But the Bible also says, 'Ye are the temple of the living God' (II Cor. 6:16). As believers we are always living in God's temple. We are to think of ourselves as serving God daily, in the temple of our bodies, and to do this we must so live as to be usable to Him."

The Christian does not drink because he knows the Lord Jesus Christ personally and is a member of His family. The Christian is a king and a priest, and the Bible specifically says that kings and priests are not to drink.

The matter of total abstinence, then, depends upon our love for the Lord Jesus Christ.

How much do we love Him?

Part II

FIVE WAYS TO HELP THE ALCOHOLIC

INTRODUCTION

EVERY PROBLEM OF MAN has a spiritual solution. The ever increasing problem of alcoholism is no exception. God has provided a way of escape. Those who are trying to help alcoholics must believe this. Otherwise, trying to counsel an alcoholic or having a member of one's family ensnared with alcohol addiction can be a frustrating experience. The situation is so complex, so staggering that there seems to be no solution apart from belief that God has provided a way of escape.

The road to rehabilitation of an alcoholic may be long and difficult, but there is hope. First, we must come to understand the alcoholic and the product that has enslaved him. Then we need to inform ourselves about the ways in which he can be helped. Whether we are working in a rescue mission, or as a pastor or counselor, or whether we are in a family situation where our hearts are broken because of the alcohol addiction of one of our loved ones, there are five definite ways in which we can help the alcoholic. We will consider these in detail in the next five chapters.

1

UNTAPPED RESOURCES

A FATHER had just stumbled into his home and was sprawled on the floor in a drunken stupor. A concerned wife knelt beside him, threw her body across his, and in anguish cried out in prayer. "God, deliver him from the power of drink. Make him a decent husband and father again. I commend him to Thee in the name of Christ!"

A widow with two small children, she had married this man after his first wife had died, leaving him with three children. For several years they were very happy—until drink began to get its claws into Clarence.

In time they were separated and the wife, following the advice of well-meaning friends and going against her own judgment, divorced him. He went off into the never-never land of the alcoholic in a helpless, hopeless, self-centered search for one bottle after another.

It was twelve years before she saw Clarence again. This time, he was sober and a respected member of the community. He was on the staff of the rescue mission where he had found Christ as his Saviour. It was our privilege to remarry them.

"I prayed for Clarence's salvation for twelve years," she told me. "I *knew* he was going to become a Christian. I kept asking God to save him."

Some three years or so before they met again and were re-married she heard that he had become a Christian.

"My prayers changed, then," she continued. "I thanked God for saving Clarence and delivering him from the power of drink. I started to pray that we might be reunited if that was God's plan for our lives."

The first way to help the alcoholic is to pray for him.

"You can do more than pray after you've prayed," S. D. Gordon says in his book *Quiet Talks on Prayer,* "but you cannot do more than pray until you have prayed."

There is no area in which this statement is more true than in working with the alcoholic. There is much that can be done for him, but we cannot successfully do anything until we have committed the individual into the hands of the Lord.

"Our prayer," Mr. Gordon explains in the same book, "is God's opportunity to get into the world which shut Him out."

Put the alcoholic on your prayer list and pray for him by name daily, believing that God is going to deliver him. The most powerful weapon we have is prayer. Because it is so powerful, we must know how to handle it.

Prayer is so important because the alcoholic is one person who cannot be helped unless he wants to be. He must ask for help before anything can be done for him. All we can do is try to bring him to the place where he wants help and will cooperate with the help he gets. The first step in accomplishing this is through prayer.

There are a few ground rules we must understand and follow if our prayer lives are going to be successful.

BE SURE YOU ARE A MEMBER OF GOD'S FAMILY

Prayer is a privilege and duty of the children of God.

When the disciples asked the Lord Jesus to teach them to pray, He said, "When ye pray, say, Our Father which art in heaven, . . ." (Luke 11:2).

So, if our prayers are going to be effective, we must first determine our relationship with the Lord Jesus Christ. Have we experienced a personal deliverance from sin through faith in Christ? Have we been born into the family of God? If we have, we know that we have a right to pray to God as our heavenly Father.

STAND ON GOD'S PROMISE TO ANSWER PRAYER

It is good to consider again what the Word of God has to say about prayer and answers to prayer in order that our faith might be strengthened.

"Therefore I say unto you, What things soever ye desire, when ye pray, believe that ye receive them, and ye shall have them" (Mark 11:24).

"And I say unto you, Ask, and it shall be given you; seek, and ye shall find; knock, and it shall be opened unto you" (Luke 11:9).

We can know that God will hear and answer our cries because He has told us so in His Word. Always remember that nothing is impossible with God.

In Houston, Texas, Art Lock was a rascal until he found Christ as his Saviour.

"For twenty years my mother prayed for me fifteen hundred miles away in Lodi, California," he wrote. "In 1950 she prayed that God would send some other mother's lost, wayward boy to her door so she could feed him, pray for him and lead him to Christ in my stead . . . Seven times men came to her door and she was able to lead them to Christ. Each time when the men were gone she prayed, 'Please, God, send someone to talk to my boy.'

"The seventh man was killed by a train the night after he knelt and accepted the Lord in her living room.

"That was in August, 1951 and—for some reason—he was

the last man who came to her door. As Christmas approached, she asked God to send her a postcard saying I had been saved.

"December 24, 1951, my aunt brought the mail to mother, saying, 'There's nothing here except a dirty old postcard addressed to you. I can hardly read it.'

"Mother seized the card and read, 'Your prayers have been answered. I have been saved. I am coming home. BUSTER.'"

Art Lock had been saved in prison in October of the same year after having been arrested for the two-hundredth time. A mother's prayer was answered.

"God does nothing but in answer to prayer," John Wesley said many, many years ago.

MAKE THE RIGHT APPROACH

The Scriptures speak of both public and private prayer. We need to observe both kinds of prayer as we pray for the alcoholic.

Private prayer, getting alone with God, should be a daily practice, preferably in the morning. It is by regular, private prayer that we keep ourselves in a right relationship with God so that He can answer our prayers. In private prayer we confess our outbursts of temper, our envy and jealousy and pride, and ask God to take them from us. It is as we confess our sins that God cleanses us and makes us suitable channels for answered prayer.

"Behold, the Lord's hand is not shortened that it cannot save; neither his ear heavy, that it cannot hear: But your iniquities have separated between you and your God, and your sins have hid his face from you, that he will not hear" (Isaiah 59:1-2).

Sin in our lives will keep God from answering our prayers. If we expect our prayers to be answered we must honestly search our hearts and lives to see if we have a right heart attitude. There is no better place to do this than in our private prayers and devotions.

Tom Hare, who is known in America as the Praying Plumber of Lisburn, Ireland, was speaking in a church in this country when several women came to him at the close of the service and asked him to pray for their husbands. That night on his knees he realized, even as he prayed, that the heart attitude of the women was wrong. The next day he called them together.

"You've asked me to pray for your husbands," he said, "but you have a selfish attitude. You want them sober so you'll have more money and an easier life. You're not interested in their salvation."

The women realized this and confessed that they had selfish reasons for wanting their husbands to give up alcohol. Once they had made their confessions, a wonderful thing happened. Their husbands, who hadn't been to church for years, began to attend the special meetings. One by one, they found Christ as their Saviour. By the time the series of meetings was over, all these men had become Christians.

They began to come together for fellowship, forming a little chapter of Alcoholics Victorious. Each time they were together they spent a period interceding with God for the souls of their former drinking buddies.

Just as that group of women had to examine themselves and confess the sin in their lives, and ask God to blot it out, so must we do the same before God will work in the life of our loved one.

Public prayer is most commonly practiced in the prayer meeting at church. In public prayers, a group of Christians share mutual burdens and pray together for a given problem or a certain situation. In Matthew 18:19 Christ makes a special promise to answer the prayers of those who get together to petition Him for a certain purpose.

It has always seemed to me that there is a special blessing when we humble ourselves enough in a prayer meeting to ask for prayer for a loved one by name. Few people will remember to pray for an "unspoken prayer request" in the days to come. Many will become concerned and pray for the loved one or friend of a fellow Christian.

"Nothing seemed to happen in the life of our wayward daughter who was rapidly becoming an alcoholic," a father said, "until I was so burdened in prayer meeting one night that I cried out to God for her by name. There was a marked change from that moment on. Not in her; the change in her came later. But people told us they were praying for her and for my wife and me. There was real concern in the congregation. The burden became easier to bear, and in time she gave her heart to Christ."

Both private and public prayer can be intercessory prayer.

"God forbid that I should sin against the Lord in ceasing to pray for you" (I Samuel 12:23). In this type of prayer we intercede before God for others. The Bible urges us to pray for one another. In the Old Testament, godly Samuel viewed failure to pray for the nation of Israel as a sin. He said, "God forbid that I should sin against the Lord in ceasing to pray for you" (I Samuel 12:23). The need of the nation was a call to prayer. The need of the alcoholic is our call to intercessory prayer. In intercessory prayer we make known before God all the details we know of a particular person or problem, and we ask Him to move in that particular situation.

I have found intercessory prayer a most valuable tool when counseling with the alcoholic. So often it is difficult for him to express himself. He has trouble saying what is on his mind and his heart. Very seldom do you get down to the very truth of the problem on the first or second interview.

I have found, however, that it's very profitable to pray for that individual at every interview, to lift him into the hands of the Lord and petition God to deliver him. The method I use might not be best for everyone. Each person should proceed in the way that makes him feel most at ease. At the close of the interview, I reach out to shake hands with the individual. While I have his hand in mine I say, "Let's pray." Right then I pray for him in Jesus' name.

And surprising things happen. I find that sometimes the person completely breaks down after I have committed him and his problem to the Lord. When that happens, I have an opportunity to get to the very crux of the matter. Often the individual will ask God for a new life through Jesus Christ.

So, if God provides the opportunity for counseling with an alcoholic, don't forget to pray for him at the close of the interview.

Sometimes the family of the alcoholic feels a real guilt complex. They ask themselves, "Have I done the right thing? Have I done all I could have done? Why did I lose my temper and talk so terribly that I drove him back to the bottle?" Families who have such a guilt complex can and should have victory over it.

In the first place, most of the temper spectacles staged by the alcoholic's family come about only after grave provocation. It is not easy to live with an alcohol addict or work with him. And we do have our human frailties which cause us, if pressed hard enough, to explode in fits of anger.

But there is no need for justifying our actions. We can confess our sins and failures to God, and be sure of His forgiveness, even as our alcoholic can have the past wiped away if he confesses his sin.

Whether we have failed or succeeded in the past makes no difference at all. We must start where we are and go on from there. So, if we have a guilt complex we should bring it to the Lord and leave it there, and enjoy the freedom and peace that come with complete forgiveness.

Members of the alcoholic's family find, when they begin to pray for him, that in certain areas they have unknowingly and unwittingly made a contribution to the drinking of the individual. They also discover areas in which they, too, have been selfish and self-centered.

I remember a certain husband and wife who came to see me at my office. The husband told me he had gone back to drinking after being free from it for some time. I talked with him, explaining that he had to turn his entire life over to God; that there was an area in which he did not have victory; a particular sore spot that caused him to explode into another drink. "You are going to have to search your heart, be honest before God, and ask Him to deliver you."

Then the woman spoke up and said tearfully, "I have to pray too. I haven't done the things he has done, but my sins are just as black. I have to turn *my* life completely to God, too."

This broke the husband. They fell on their knees and prayed together. What a wonderful experience that was!

As far as I know today, this couple is living together happily somewhere in Wisconsin, their home free from the awful curse of alcoholism.

REMEMBER, YOU ARE THE SUPPLY LINE

It is important that we constantly keep before us the picture of ourselves as a channel of God's power. Our hearts are burdened because of the terrible curse that has taken hold of our alcoholic. We cry out to God. That sets the forces of Almighty God to work. He sends His power by the Holy Spirit to us and through us to that individual.

Now, we don't see this power radiating through us and we can't feel it, but this is the way it works.

We may be sure God is interested in this problem. He loves this person more than we do. As we pray, we cooperate with God in bringing His purposes to pass. We should not beg God. However, after we've asked Him to bring deliverance to the individual, we should begin to thank Him that He is going to do what we have asked. We must believe with all our hearts that God is going to work, and trust Him to work.

This is not easy. We have been suffering for such a long while under the curse alcoholism brings that we are impatient for God to work. We pray, and when nothing seems to happen immediately, we begin to get discouraged, and our doubts grow.

A sort of chain reaction sets in. Discouragement causes us to fail to thank God that He is answering prayer. We get careless, then, about naming the individual before the Lord in prayer.

Times without number people have come into my office, their faces lined with weariness and doubt, who say something like this: "I've gotten to the place where I'm tired of praying. God isn't going to answer."

I can well understand how they feel. All of us have to fight against the *sin* of discouragement. For that is just what discouragement is—sin.

The moment we become discouraged and stop thanking God ahead of time for answering our prayers and begin to neglect praying for the alcoholic we are so concerned about, we will lose our effectiveness as prayer helpers. God has to turn His attention to us and work with us, moving in our hearts and lives by His Spirit to get us to see our sin.

Perhaps some other sin besides lack of faith and discouragement is blocking the channel and hindering answers to our prayers—hatred, an unforgiving spirit, the wrong heart attitude.

Once in a while men come into the Mission whom we would just as soon write off and have nothing to do with. I remember one particular fellow who felt that he had been cheated in the settlement of an accident claim and had made up his mind he wasn't going to work the rest of his life.

He was at the Mission when a crew from a local TV station came down to do a program about the Mission. As usual, they were free to interview anyone they wished without the presence of Mission personnel, and this man was among those interviewed.

A couple of days later the TV producer called me to his office and asked me to listen to the tape. All the man's bitterness poured out in a tirade against me personally, the Open Door Mission in particular, and rescue missions in general.

I was furious.

Then God began to convict me of my attitude toward this fellow. I confessed it and began to pray that God would deliver him from the bonds of sin. But I still didn't think I wanted to have any part of working with him.

God dealt with me about that, too. I had confessed my wrong attitude and I was praying for the man's salvation, but I am not sure I really wanted what I was praying for. At any rate, I didn't want it badly enough to be willing to deal with the man myself. I began to pray that if God wanted me to talk with Him He would send him around again.

God did just that.

It wasn't easy for me when the man came into my office for counseling. The bitterness and hatred I thought I had put aside welled up within me once more. My feelings were a reaction to the man's warped philosophy that the world owed him a living and he wasn't going to work another day in his life, for I strongly believe that a man should not eat if he does not work.

I had to confess to God once more my unwillingness to witness to him and to ask Him for the victory I needed to

talk with this man intelligently. Until that moment I hadn't
honestly wanted what I had been praying for.

I wish I could report to you that he accepted Christ as his
Saviour, but that hasn't happened yet, as far as we know.
However, he is working and holding down a job, and the
relationship between the two of us is good. We are still praying for him, confident that one of these days he is going to
accept Christ.

DID YOU ASK?

In a way, it seems strange that we must ask God before He
will answer, but that is another principle of prayer. It is
true that God knows our every need, even before we ask. It
is also true that God says we should ask in order to receive.
"And all things, whatsoever ye shall ask in prayer, believing,
ye shall receive" (Matthew 21:22). Now, that is a positive
promise from God. If we ask, we are going to receive. So,
we must ask.

But we must know what we are asking for. Is what we
want according to God's will? I am quite sure that is the
reason our Blessed Lord insists that we talk these things over
with Him. As we sit down with Him and talk things over
with Him, we submit our wills to His will. And we present
with confidence any petition that is according to His will.

Not so long ago a business acquaintance of mine was having
some real business problems. I asked him, "Have you ever
talked to God about this?"

"I'm not sure I understand what you mean."

"If you went to a bank to get a loan you'd talk it over with
the banker, wouldn't you? You would have to give him a
list of your assets and liabilities. You'd have to explain to
him the business potential you saw in the future. In short,
you would have to take this banker into your confidence because he would need to know certain things about you and

your business if he were to make you a business loan. Isn't that true?"

He replied after a few moments of thought, "I suppose so."

"That's what God means when He tells us to ask Him for things in prayer," I continued. "Why don't you get your books out and make up a statement and read it before God, and let Him in on your business. Then ask God for the things you need—money, better employee relations, a better location, or any other need. Talk your problems over with God."

When I walked into his office a month or two later, he reminded me of our conversation.

"I did just what you suggested," he said. "I got my books and made my statement and read it off before God. You know, it is wonderful the way things have happened and how God is managing this business and making it a success."

Perhaps you need to do the same thing in praying for your alcoholic.

Are You Expecting an Answer?

Are you honestly expecting an answer? Or have you allowed doubts to cloud your heart so that you go through the motions of prayer, but without any real assurance that God even hears? Doubt is like a canker, a great hindrance to prayer. Doubt is sin and must be judged and confessed.

The chief reason we doubt is that we don't realize exactly who we are dealing with. Our minds accept the fact that God is great, that He is all-powerful, that He can change the life of an individual or the course of any series of circumstances.

But our hearts don't believe it. If they did, doubts would not destroy our peace of mind and blight our prayer life.

We must stop and consider how great God is!

"Are there any among the vanities of the Gentiles that can cause rain? or can the heavens give showers? art not thou he,

O LORD our God? therefore we will wait upon thee: for thou hast made all these things" (Jeremiah 14:22).

He created the Heavens and the earth out of nothing. The mountains and desert wastes and mighty oceans are His handiwork. He orders the affairs of men. He moves against nations to work out His will.

This is the God to whom we pray. This is the God who urges us to make our requests known to Him. "Be careful for nothing; but in everything by prayer and supplication with thanksgiving let your requests be made known unto God. And the peace of God, which passeth all understanding, shall keep your hearts and minds through Christ Jesus" (Philippians 4:6-7).

How can we doubt our mighty, all-powerful God?

Statistics tend to prove that an individual in his twenties is more difficult to reach than one who is thirty-five or forty years old. They say the alcoholic who has been jailed for drunkenness a number of times is a better risk than the alcoholic addict who has been jailed for some criminal offense. Such a man, they say, seldom comes to seek help.

And with 75 percent of all crime committed by individuals who are under the influence of beverage alcohol, we can safely conclude that there are a lot of such men around. Some of these are men who have been released from prison on parole after having committed some crime or crimes. Humanly speaking, men like that would appear to be hopeless, but they aren't. God makes the difference!

Why God would want to answer the prayers of weaklings like us I do not know, but how I praise Him that He does.

"But God hath chosen the foolish things of the world to confound the wise; and God hath chosen the weak things of the world to confound the things which are mighty; and base things of the world, and things which are despised, hath God

chosen, yea, and things which are not, to bring to nought
things that are" (I Corinthians 1:27-28).

God can take nothing and use it to bring to nought that
which is. How comforting that should be to each of us
who is praying for an alcoholic! It doesn't make any difference
how long the individual has been an alcoholic or how bad the
situation is. God is on the throne. He is able to take that
helpless, hopeless individual and restore him completely as
a useful member of society.

An Editorial Prayer, Prohibition and the Liquor Industry

People are often disturbed about the tremendous problem
facing America today. They ask, for example, "What can we
do about social drinking? How can we curb the advertising
that is directed so pointedly at the housewife?"

The trend of current liquor ads is disturbing. They are
aimed at persuading the housewife, who does more than 80
percent of the buying, to bring alcoholic beverages into the
home, thus making a cocktail lounge out of the living room
and a saloon out of the basement recreation room.

Other questions asked are: "Is prohibition the answer?
Can we get a liquor law through Congress?"

From a practical standpoint it doesn't seem wise to spend
valuable time and effort fighting an industry that has made
12 billion dollars in the last year and spent more than 400
million in advertising to increase their business. There isn't
a Christian or temperance organization in the world that can
raise the amount of money necessary to push a bill of stringent
control through Congress, to say nothing of battling a prohibition amendment through Congress and the required
state Legislatures or conventions.

But there is a power available that is greater than any
power in all the earth. There is a power available that can

dry up the liquor industry—not through legal action, but through spiritual action. There is a power that can deliver men from the addiction of sin and bring them into the freedom of salvation.

This power is prayer.

The only effective tool we have at our disposal that the liquor industry can never buy and can never destroy is the power of united prayer that people might be delivered from the damning influence of the misuse of beverage alcohol.

Recently I had the privilege of listening to a speech by Abraham Vereide, founder of International Christian Leadership, the organization that sponsors the presidential prayer breakfast, the governors' prayer breakfasts, the prayer breakfast in our Congress and Senate, and which sponsors prayer breakfasts among businessmen all over the world. Mr. Vereide told of the way his work got started in Seattle, Washington. He told of a concerted effort on the part of corrupt political forces to take over the state. There was a great political crisis.

"We began to pray," he said. "There were nineteen in the group and only one was a Christian. But the others were interested in learning the answer to this tremendous political problem. As the men began to read the Word of God they got straightened out personally. As that happened, they were able to be channels of prayer. They went about this quietly and secretly."

In their prayer meetings God seemed to lay on their hearts certain things they should do, such as getting people out to vote, precinct by precinct. Through them God changed the course of that election and, as a result, changed the course of politics in the State of Washington.

From that beginning the prayer breakfasts were born, prayer breakfasts that have changed the complexion of politics in certain instances and have changed the lives of important

men so that God has been able to work through them to
change the nature of politics in some areas.

The Bible tells us that we have an obligation to pray for
men in authority (I Timothy 2:1-4). If we have the same
concern with regard to beverage alcohol and the liquor
industry which those nineteen men in Seattle had for their
state, and if we begin to meet in little groups to pray about
this burden, we will see things happen. God may even deliver
the nation from the clutches of the liquor industry and as a
result deliver our families, our young people and the alcoholics. He will begin to work miracles as we get right with
Him and become channels through which He can work.

Pray.

2

PRESENTING THE GOSPEL

I KNOW what the gospel of Christ was able to do for me when I was in a Texas prison in 1948, and I know what He is doing in my life every day. I have seen how He has worked in the lives of men and women in all stages of society, snatching them from the relentless grip of alcohol addiction and making them free.

"Religion can be a tremendous force in the rehabilitation of an alcoholic," Miss Phyllis Snyder of Chicago's highly successful Alcoholic Treatment Center said.

Paul speaks in even stronger terms: "The gospel of Christ . . . is the power of God unto salvation to every one that believeth; to the Jew first, and also to the Greek" (Romans 1:16).

FIRST THINGS FIRST

When we first consider the problem of alcoholism and make an attempt to understand the alcoholic, we are apt to be overwhelmed by it. The problem is so bewildering and has so many ramifications we scarcely know where to begin. We feel like we are in a maze, and we find it easy to forget that the most important thing we can do for the alcoholic is to present the gospel to him.

To be sure, it isn't always possible to preach the gospel to every man on every occasion. You can't preach to an individual if he is in a drunken stupor or if he needs medical attention. But we must always keep our attention focused on this one fact: the most important thing we can do for the alcohol addict is to present the gospel to him at the earliest possible moment.

My associate, Garland Thompson, who is the founder and superintendent of the Open Door Mission in Omaha, taught me this. He has never been an alcoholic, nor has he made a special study of alcoholism. His entire life has been devoted to prayer and personal witnessing.

I have seen Garland put an arm around a man who is too drunk to talk, telling him that God loves him and praying for him before he sends him on his way to sober up or, perhaps, to get medical attention. I have had the privilege of talking to some of those same men after they were won to Christ. I've had men tell me gratefully, "Know what set me to thinking? It was Garland Thompson putting his arm around me and telling me that God loves me and, because He loves me, you guys here at the Mission were going to help me. I was pretty drunk, but that got through to me."

It was Christ who worked the victory in the lives of such men (and women), freeing them from alcoholism. In my own experience, it was the gospel of the Lord Jesus Christ that got hold of me after everything else had failed. If your alcoholic is to be delivered, you must present the gospel to him.

This may not always be easy. A good friend of mine with an alcoholic brother found that to be true. "I've had all of you I can take!" his brother snarled at him.

An attorney discouraged him when he mentioned trying to get help for his brother through the gospel. The attorney scornfully said, "If the psychiatrists and trained people at the state hospital weren't able to help him, I'm sure your religious friend wouldn't be able to help."

As the "religious friend," I wasn't able to help personally, but I was able to point the young alcoholic to the One who could solve all his problems. Today he is a stalwart Christian.

A PASTOR'S REMINDER

Working with alcoholics is not the most enjoyable part of a pastor's ministry. The alcoholic is difficult, surly, and uncooperative. Usually, he thinks that anyone who tries to help him is a personal enemy. He is secretive, untruthful, and suspicious, and is apt to be involved in immorality, the writing of bad checks, and gambling. His excessive and compulsive drinking has deeply hurt and affected the lives of—on an average—five innocent persons. He has become a blight on his family and his community.

The average pastor has gone through some difficult experiences with alcoholics—experiences similar to those I have had.

For instance, there was the time I was called to the home of a man who had fallen against the french doors in his living room. His arms were badly cut when they went through the glass, and he was standing in the middle of the living room floor, blood running in puddles on the white rug he was standing on. He was in a drunken rage, his terrified daughters were sobbing in the bedroom, and his wife was shouting at him in anger, scarcely mindful of the fact that he had been hurt.

Another time I was called to the home of a lovely family in a very nice neighborhood of our city. What I found was anything but lovely. The older son, who had lost his wife because of alcoholism, seemed bent on drinking himself to death. The stench in the room he had refused to leave for a number of days was terrible, and the filth was something I can't quite put into words. It wasn't easy to be in that room nor to see the hurt that gleamed in his Christian mother's eyes and the mute agony on the face of his sister, who also knew Christ as her Saviour.

When we get into a situation like that it is sometimes difficult to remember that God is all-powerful and that Jesus Christ, through the power of the gospel, can change the life of a man.

Pastors as well as mission workers need to continually realize in a very personal way that God does love the alcoholic and that we who are His ambassadors must love the alcoholic, too.

"But God commendeth his love toward us, in that, while we were yet sinners, Christ died for us" (Romans 5:8).

This applies to the alcohol addict, too. We need to be reminded of that and the fact that men are saved from the horrors of alcoholism and are brought to a place of respectability and service by the gospel of Christ.

Stan Collie was such a man. He had degenerated to the point where, at forty years of age, his wife and six children went hungry so he could have something to drink. On Saturday night his wife and a couple of the older youngsters would go down to the business district of the roaring little northern Saskatchewan community where they lived, to pick him out of the gutter and pull him home in a coaster wagon.

Stan was undoubtedly as bad as most of the cases that come to pastors, and the problems his drinking caused were just as great.

Then Christ got hold of him. His life was transformed. He began to witness to others, and today he is known as the founder of the Northern Canada Evangelical Mission, an organization that has become a great force for God with more than one hundred and twenty missionaries all across Canada. We should look upon each man as an opportunity.

Another reason we pastors often are reluctant to work with the alcoholic is the amount of time it takes.

"You have to throw the clock away when you're dealing with the alcoholic," Charles Morey of the Chicago Christian Industrial League said. "It is probably the most time-consuming type of counseling."

With the responsibilities of a pastorate today, it is very difficult for a minister to give one man the amount of time he should have in order to help him out of alcoholism. For that reason, it is often wise to form a team of concerned men in the church to work with the individual alcohol addicts. We will go into that in greater detail in the chapter on fellowship.

GOD'S WAY IS BASIC

Dr. E. N. Jellinek, one of the world's foremost experts in the field of alcoholism, in his study on alcohol addiction and chronic alcoholism, noted that a most interesting finding was that the need for religious security and standards rated so highly in overcoming alcoholism.

A pamphlet on alcoholism published by the Yale Center of Alcohol Studies reaches the same conclusion. "The number of addictive drinkers who have been helped to attain permanent abstinence by the means of religious approaches is probably far greater than is usually suspected."

Clifford J. Earle, author of *How to Help an Alcoholic*, says, "Religion is a major aid in the treatment of alcoholism. Christ is not just another alcoholic therapy, however, as though one could choose between a religious or a psychiatric treatment. Instead, it is an approach that takes into account the spiritual aspects of personality and religious resources for successful living."

We can only stand back and wonder at the grace of God.

CHRISTIANITY IS A LIFE TO LIVE

I have found that an alcoholic may have to go all the way

to the bottom, and sometimes onto skid row, because he has
not seen the Christian life demonstrated.

"Everyone talks a good game when it comes to this Christian life," one alcoholic said to me with keen perception,
"but I don't see anyone playing it very well."

There are times when I cannot help wondering if such
failure in Christian living isn't a big hindrance in many cases.

One such situation came to us at the Mission not long ago.
The husband—we'll call him Pete—had a relationship with
his church but had not taken Christ as his Saviour. The
wife, Sue, was a Christian; she had gotten some Bible training
and had been a home missionary for several years before their
marriage. Pete, who had become an alcoholic, came to me
for counseling. I tried to talk with him about the things of
the Lord, but it was hard for him to understand what I was
talking about.

When an alcoholic has a family available to turn to, it is
usually wise for the counselor to take the whole family into
consideration. So we began to give special attention to Sue.

We had noticed during the time when Pete fell back to
drinking that she had a very definite spiritual lack—a lack of
dependency upon the Lord. Salvation she could understand.
In fact, she was well versed in the Scriptures and domineered
her husband in their family devotions and harped on salvation until Pete rebelled against the very mention of the word.
But she did not live up to what she preached. She had no
understanding of how to live a victorious Christian life. Nor
did she seem to know that God could give her victory over
her problems and troubles.

"I might not know much about the Bible," Pete told me,
"but if I'm going to be free from alcoholism, I've got to have
something better than my wife has. As a matter of fact, if
what she's got is religion, I know that religion is not the
answer to my problem."

After a time we were able to help him to see things in their right perspective, and he came to a saving knowledge of the Lord Jesus Christ.

Then he began to live the Christian life, took over the leadership in their home, and gave the Word of God its rightful place in their home, as he should have done all along. Then he was able to help his very weak, insecure wife in a number of areas in her life. She is a better Christian today because her husband knows the Lord.

When we talk with an alcohol addict about the Lord Jesus Christ, we must be very careful that we ourselves understand that this is a life to live, not a theology to be expounded.

We can teach Sunday school, harp continually on religion, keep a Bible in the most prominent place in the house, and have devotions regularly. Yet, if we are not living victorious Christian lives, we cannot hope to reach our alcoholic.

"What you are," Emerson wrote, "speaks so loudly I cannot hear a word you say."

We should prayerfully strive to live in such a way that the alcoholic will look at us and say to himself, "I want what that person has."

CHRISTIANITY IS A NEW LIFE

A truth we should always be careful to point up to the alcoholic who is making a profession of faith is that faith in Christ means a new life. "Therefore, if any man be in Christ, he is a new creature; old things are passed away; behold, all things are become new" (II Corinthians 5:17).

Salvation is a ticket to Heaven, that is true. Much of the New Testament deals with salvation, and some of the most important passages of Scripture explain how one might obtain it. We cannot minimize the importance of salvation. Yet, all too often we have made it the place where our Christian experience ends, and it is nothing of the sort. When a man is saved, he is born again. This new birth marks the beginning of a new and entirely different life. But that life is to grow and develop and mature.

This truth presents a tremendous appeal to the alcoholic. He has made such a terrible mess of his old life that he's reached the end of the road. The dirty, tangled skein of his past could never be untangled and knit into anything new. A new life is the only answer for his situation.

"And along with this gift comes the realization that God wants us to turn from godless living and from sinful pleasures and to live good, God-fearing lives, day after day, looking forward to that time when His glory shall be seen— the glory of our great God and Saviour Jesus Christ, who died under God's judgment against our sins, so that He could rescue us from constant falling into sin, and make us His very own people, with cleansed hearts and real enthusiasm for doing kind things for others" (Titus 2:12-14, *Living Letters*).

The grace of God provides more than deliverance from the punishment our sins deserved, more than a leisurely journey into Heaven. God's grace gives the believing sinner a completely new life.

When we talk with a new Christian it is wise to talk with him about taking a personal inventory, listing his bad and good qualities and asking God to take over in the areas where he needs help.

We should also urge him to feed on God's Word and to pray every morning. The best advice ever given to me was written to me on a postcard by a Christian who belonged to the Gideons, an organization which places Bibles in hotel rooms. This person wrote, "Spend fifteen minutes a day reading your Bible and fifteen minutes a day in prayer. If you start your day that way, you'll keep true to the Lord and grow in Him."

When we present the gospel of the Lord Jesus Christ to

the individual we must be careful not to present a limited view of salvation. When we present the truth that Christianity is a new life, we give the alcoholic something to which to cling. He will see that God is genuinely interested in him and will provide him with all that he needs. God has given him a new life which can be molded and shaped after Christ!

What a glorious hope!

3

FELLOWSHIP

IT IS STRANGE that fellowship should be so important
in an area where it is so difficult to give what is implied by
fellowship—communion, intimacy, joint interest, and feeling.
It is not easy for anyone involved with an alcoholic to give
him fellowship.

How does a wife who has been beaten in a brutish, drunken
rage forget such treatment? How does a wife put aside the
ugly fact of her husband's infidelity? Can a mother forget
that her children have been neglected and abused? Can a
pastor or a counselor ignore the fact that an individual has
caused so much anguish to so many innocent people?

Yet Alcoholics Anonymous, the most successful organization involved in the treatment of the alcoholic, has made
fellowship a cornerstone in their efforts to help the individual.
We must do the same, no matter how difficult, if we are
going to help our alcoholic.

Of course, fellowship is a two-way street. It must be
offered, received, and returned. The alcohol addict has an
important part to play in fellowship if it is going to be
effective in helping him back to sobriety.

That is one of the keys to the AA program. Fellowship is
offered, but is never forced on the individual. If he wants it,
they stand ready to help him. If he doesn't, there is nothing
they can do.

106

When a call from an alcoholic comes to a city's central AA office, one or two AA volunteers who are making the "twelve steps" call on him that night to talk to him. They tell him about the AA program, what it has done for them, and what it can do for him. They don't berate him. They don't sulk and refuse to talk. They offer him fellowship. It is entirely up to him whether he accepts their fellowship or not.

If he wants help, they will try to help him in every way possible. If medical care or hospitalization is necessary they will try to get it for him. They will do what they can to help him through the awful throes of alcohol withdrawal.

They will invite him to an AA meeting. If he comes, he will be welcomed and will be made to feel at home. So, if he continues to respond to the fellowship that is offered, AA will be able to continue helping him.

However, fellowship must be offered to the individual in every area of life. This must be remembered and practiced by the pastor or counselor, and by members of the individual's family. We must understand his problem and realize that he is suffering from addiction. We must learn to create an atmosphere of fellowship for him and give him encouragement to desire sobriety more than drink. We must offer him respect and dignity, and opportunity to take his place as a respected member of society.

If we are going to be able to offer fellowship to an individual who has such a warped, self-centered personality that he has been living only for another drink, we need something outside ourselves to enable us to do it. We need a strong, abiding faith in Christ and the strength He can give.

When I was on the counseling staff at the Nebraska State Penitentiary, a certain prisoner asked to see me. I was given his "rap sheet" (in dignified terminology, his case history). All the crimes he had been convicted of were listed, including the offense for which he was sentenced the last time.

"What a character this guy is!" I thought.

Yet, as I talked with him, he seemed sincere in his desire for help, and I had the privilege of leading him to personally acknowledge Christ as his Saviour. As I watched him leave the room after the interview, I said to myself, "I wonder if he'll make it."

Instantly the Lord rebuked me, and I had to ask myself, "How did you make it? You were in prison when you accepted Christ. Your record might not have been as long as this fellow's, but it was just as black. You were no better than he is. How did you make it?"

There is only one answer. I made it because God took over in my life. He gave me the encouragement and strength I needed. He sent concerned Christians my way to help me. He would do the same with this individual.

Whenever I am faced with a difficult case, I am constantly reminded that nothing is too hard for God, "Who will have all men to be saved and come to a knowledge of repentance" (I Timothy 2:4).

We must have the attitude that God is interested in every individual and that we can offer fellowship to our alcoholic.

Generally accepted is the idea that it takes an alcoholic to help an alcoholic, that you have to be one to understand one. Though I personally have suffered from alcohol addiction, I do not have rapport with the alcoholic solely because of that. Garland Thompson has rapport with the men who come stumbling into the Mission; and to my knowledge he has never taken a drink in his life.

We can have rapport with the alcoholic because we have been separated from God by sin just as he has been separated from God by sin. And we have been delivered, by Christ, from our sin, even as he can be delivered, by Christ, from his sin.

We must hold before the alcoholic the truth that Christ is

vitally interested in the sinner. "And Jesus . . . said unto them, They that are whole need not a physician; but they that are sick. I came not to call the righteous, but sinners, to repentance" (Luke 5:31-32).

We cannot isolate alcoholism as some ugly and almost unforgivable sin. We must see it as a part of the universal problem of sin. Once that is clear to us we see our alcoholic as one who has the same universal problem of sin that we, ourselves, had. We see him as a sinner who needs deliverance from a sinful nature, who needs to be born again into a new life through Jesus Christ, our Lord.

As a result, we no longer approach the problem of offering fellowship to him as a fearful thing. We no longer see him as a hideous person who brings grief and hurt to women and children, wrecking homes, destroying peace. We simply see him as a sinner in need of a Deliverer. When we see his problem in this light we are no longer afraid to attempt to cope with it.

THE SAMARITAN PRINCIPLE

The road from Jerusalem to Jericho was rocky and very dangerous, a favorite lurking place for roving bands of robbers. The nameless traveler in the story of the Good Samaritan fell into the hands of such a band. They beat him, stripped off his clothes, and robbed him, leaving him half dead.

The twentieth century alcoholic is also traveling a rough and rocky road. The thieves of alcoholic beverages have robbed him of his job, his home, and his family and stripped him of his self-respect. He has very few friends in a world that condemns him because of his addiction.

In the Bible story, when the Good Samaritan came along, he had compassion for the man who had been so shamefully treated. Sorrow for the suffering of this poor fellow welled in his heart. He had such concern and love for him that he did something about it. He bound up the injured man's wounds.

We, too, must have the compassion and love of the Good Samaritan, if we are going to offer fellowship to our alcoholic. When we first see this poor, broken hulk of a man there is a very good chance that he is going to need medical attention. We may have to see that he is treated by a doctor, possibly even going into the hospital or a treatment center. Often in treatment centers and rescue missions the individual must go through a long period of physical adjustment before any spiritual or mental therapy can be given.

The next thing the Samaritan did was to put the injured man on his own mount and take him to the inn where he requested that the injured man be cared for. The Samaritan became personally involved by dressing the injured man's wounds, by bringing him to the inn, and by offering payment for his care until he returned.

I shall never forget the first alcoholic I worked with after entering the ministry. He would come to the parsonage at two or three o'clock in the morning and get us out of bed. One night by the time I got him steady enough to take him home and put him to bed, it was five in the morning. I was disgusted. I knelt in my study and talked with the Lord about him.

"I'm never going to have anything more to do with this fellow, Lord. He won't assume any of the responsibilities of his business or do anything his family asks him to do. He won't do anything I ask him to. He won't respond to the gospel. I'm through with him!"

Then a still, small voice seemed to speak to me. "Jerry, you're going to have John on your back until he is free." That is exactly the way it worked out.

You see, when we work with an alcoholic it is necessary that we work with him on an individual basis, as one person to another. We must not weaken or falter until the individual is delivered.

Not only is it difficult to offer fellowship to our alcoholic but it costs something. Like the Good Samaritan, we must be willing to pay the price. We're going to have to pay the price of time, money, and our own personal convenience. And the price paid will seem small compared to the joy of seeing our alcoholic delivered from his chains and restored to a place of respect and dignity in the family, church, and community.

PROBLEMS IN OFFERING FELLOWSHIP

Fellowship must be a team project if our alcoholic is to be helped to a life of total abstinence and permanent sobriety. It must come from the family, the church, friends, and associates. The first place the alcoholic should expect fellowship—at home—is usually the last place it is offered.

I can hear the indignant cries of the wives and children of alcoholics: "How can I offer fellowship to him when he's hurt me so?"

The answer is found in the reply of the disciples when Christ told them they should forgive a person who had sinned against them seventy times seven times.

"Lord, increase our faith."

We cannot forgive enough to take such an individual back into fellowship without the help and strength that come from God.

Marty Mann, founder of the National Council on Alcoholism and its Executive Director since 1944, writes from personal experience in her book *Marty Mann's New Primer on Alcoholism.** One chapter is called Home Treatment.

> The "home treatment" can be divided into two main categories, words and actions, or talk and behavior. Talk

usually goes on for some time before behavior begins to bear it out. Then it continues right alongside the behavior. For purposes of clarity we will follow the line of talk through to its bitter end before taking up the behavior which usually joins it midway.

Talk, to someone whose drinking is beginning to create a problem, usually begins with "sweet reasonableness." An effort is made at friendly discussion on what drinking is doing to the drinker (such as his "lack of judgment" and "thoughtfulness"), leading up to what it is doing to his family, at which time it is apt to become a trifle acid, and sometimes ends in an all-out row. Nevertheless, the effort to discuss the matter "reasonably" is renewed over and over again, despite the fact that as time goes on it seems to lead more and more swiftly to acrimonious dispute or cold anger. The alcoholic soon calls this nagging, . . .

Emotional appeals are another form of talk frequently used. "How can you do this to me?"; "Doesn't my love mean anything to you?"; "How can you do this to the children" or "to yourself?" These point the finger of shame and blame at the alcoholic, increasing his already acute sense of guilt, and giving him another excuse to drink more, in order to "forget."

. . . .

Neither the emotional appeal nor the morality lecture ever seems to do the slightest good in bringing an alcoholic to seek help.*

Mrs. Mann goes on to state that promises and coaxing might appear to have some success at the time, but if so, it is only temporary. Extracting a promise from an alcoholic is usually a waste of time. By this time, he probably couldn't keep it if he wanted to.

The wife usually will advance to threatening the alcoholic—

---

*Marty Mann's New Primer on Alcoholism (New York: Rinehart & Co., Inc., 1958), pp. 102-3.

threatening to have him jailed or committed to an institution, but that doesn't do any good either.

I have had many distraught women come into my office whose desperate stories follow the pattern so ably outlined by Mrs. Mann.

The behavior that goes with the talk is substantially the same, too. The alcoholic hides the liquor that is kept in the house, or locks it up, or even pours it out.

"This usually proves a futile gesture," Mrs. Mann goes on, "for the alcoholic then sets his really remarkable ingenuity to getting more in, or getting himself out of the house, and to the nearest source of supply. It must be remembered that to him, his need is desperate and overwhelming; it brooks no interference, and sets up in him the blind courage of a charging bull, plus all of the cunning and cleverness of a skilled second-story man."*

There are other defense mechanisms—the withholding of money, or perhaps even reporting the tavern to the authorities for serving the alcoholic when he was already intoxicated. But these things are rarely effective. By this time the alcoholic is far gone and badly in need of treatment.

We who have had any dealings with alcoholics know how futile the type of home treatment just described actually is. We have tried it with many and varied innovations of our own. We know it doesn't work.

How, then, can we help?

HELP IN OFFERING FELLOWSHIP

The situation in which we find ourselves when we try to help our alcoholic is frustrating and takes its toll on us spiritually, mentally, and physically. If we are going to help our alcoholic, we must first get help for ourselves.

When we see a member of our family moving progressively

*P. 106 of Mrs. Mann's book.

down the seven steps to chronic alcoholism, we should go and talk with our minister, preferably, or another Christian in whom we have confidence. Not necessarily to see what can be done for our alcoholic but to help us to get a right heart attitude in meeting the problem. We need to be sure our faith in the Lord Jesus Christ is firm and strong. We need to be sure that we have a forgiving spirit, even to the point of forgiving seventy times seven times. We need to be sure that our personal relationship with Christ is such that it will allow us to take our troubled heart and mind and present them to Him to receive the assurance and strength we need to carry on.

We must have the ability and wisdom to help our alcoholic make a recovery rather than being a stumbling block.*

The fellowship of the family is very important in the alcohol addict's recovery. Still, although we may want desperately to do everything necessary in order to help, we are afraid it isn't going to work out.

Fear is a very natural thing in such circumstances. We are afraid our alcoholic is going to take another drink. We are afraid he will lie to us again. We are even afraid that he is lying to us now, and if he should be gone half an hour longer than we think he should be we immediately think the worst.

However, if we are going to help him, we have to take advantage of every sober moment. In that sober moment we

*A great deal of help can be obtained by writing to the addresses below.

National Council on Alcoholism, 2 East 103rd St., New York, 29, New York. (They also have a directory of affiliates in other cities which is available upon request.)

Al-Anon Family Group Headquarters, Inc., P.O. Box 182, Madison Square Station, New York 10, New York.

The International Union of Gospel Missions, James Moellendick, Executive Director, Parkersburg, West Virginia. (A local rescue mission affiliated with the I.U.G.M. will also supply you with material. They also have a counselor available to help those who go to them for help, referred by a pastor.)

must accept him as a normal individual: we must accept him into the family circle and routine.

The Scriptures tell us that perfect love casts out fear. First we must love our Lord and Saviour, Jesus Christ. As we love Him, we will be able to express love to our alcoholic and to trust his present sobriety.

Fear can carry within it the seeds of destruction.

We saw that in Mabel H. She agreed to be reestablished with her alcoholic husband, Don. He got a good job in another community, they bought a new home, and things were going well. But Mabel was always afraid Don was going on another drunk. And with her fear she felt shame. She was sure everybody knew he was an alcoholic and looked down on them for it.

This was imaginary. Actually, the people in the church rejoiced that he had been delivered from the sin of alcohol addiction, that their home had been restored, and that his testimony was clear and true. But Mabel wouldn't let the church draw them into fellowship. She wouldn't attend any of the church meetings and didn't want her husband to go to the men's fellowship. Because she wouldn't go to church, he wouldn't either. His fellowship with God was broken.

She made no friends and the only visitors in their home were those that they could not avoid having. Her husband was a friendly individual, and so he made friends at work, got in with the wrong group of fellows, and soon started to drink again.

If we are going to help our alcoholic, we must put fear aside and enter into normal activities with him, guiding him into associations with the right kind of friends who will help rather than hinder.

There is another factor that, although unpleasant, must be considered. Until our alcoholic is set completely free from the power of beverage alcohol, there is a good probability that he will go on another drunk. Even though this happens, we are going to have to conduct ourselves in such a way that this drunk does not interfere with our regular, normal home life. This may be one of the most difficult things we are called upon to do, but we must determine not to allow this sort of thing to interfere with our social activities.

This will help to develop an atmosphere that will make it possible for us to have the right frame of mind so we will want to continue to help our alcoholic without rancor or bitterness in our hearts. There are a number of ways in which we can help ourselves so that our hearts will be right in this difficult situation.

We should observe a regular time each morning for Bible study and prayer, taking the Psalms as a special message from God to us. Repeatedly, as we read the Psalms, we see the Psalmist lay hold of the mighty power of God, and we see God give deliverance. As God delivered David, so can He bring you through the dark days with a sweet spirit and a kindly attitude.

It may be that we will find help in joining Al-Anon, an organization of people just like ourselves, who are not alcoholics, but who have an alcoholic in our immediate families. In such an organization a person may be helped to overcome the prejudice regarding the alcoholic that can be an obstacle to our understanding and treating him successfully. Many families and friends refuse to recognize that the alcoholic is suffering from a very real problem of addiction that he must be delivered from. The alcoholic himself often doesn't recognize his addiction. Understanding this, we should be more tolerant and play our family program in such a way that our alcoholic will voluntarily accept help.

Most states provide a way of committing alcoholics for treatment, forcibly, but those who know, say that about all it does is give the family a brief period of relief. The truth is that it is impossible to help a man who does not want to be helped.

Don't make the error of thinking of an alcoholic as a weak-willed person. His will may be warped, but it is not weak. He is as stubborn as an ox. When his will is brought into line with God's will, he will not only stop drinking but will remain sober.

A wife who wishes to remain anonymous wrote an AA pamphlet setting down some suggestions for the wife of an alcoholic to guide in her treatment of him.

> 1. Never lose your temper. Even though your husband becomes unbearable and you have to leave him temporarily, do so without rancor. Patience and good temper are most necessary.
>
> 2. Never tell him what he must do about his drinking. If he gets the idea you are a nag or a killjoy, your chance of accomplishing anything useful will be zero. He will use that as an excuse to drink more. He will tell you that he is misunderstood. This may lead to lonely evenings for you. He may seek someone else to console him —and not always another man.
>
> 3. Be determined that your husband's drinking is not going to spoil your relation with your children or your friends. They need your companionship and your help. It is possible to have a full and a useful life, even though your husband continues to drink. We know women who are unafraid, even happy, under these conditions. Do not set your heart on reforming your husband. You may be unable to do so, no matter how hard you try.

Humanly speaking, it is impossible for us to have a happy life under circumstances like this. Yet we can have a victorious, happy Christian life if we put our trust in the Lord, have devotions regularly, and take an active part in the public worship of our church. "Not forsaking the assembling of yourselves together" (Hebrews 10:25).

HOW THE CHURCH CAN OFFER FELLOWSHIP

An ironic though tragic fact to be faced in the treatment of the alcoholic is that those who have the least to do with him are those who are best able to help him. So often, when an alcoholic is discovered in a congregation, the members react with condemnation, shunning him until he has "proved" himself to them. There are times when such condemnation spills over to engulf the individual's family, as well.

The church's attitude toward the individual, the way in which they accept him in fellowship or reject him, can have much to do with whether he succeeds in his struggle for sobriety.

We saw that demonstrated very graphically in two youthful alcoholics in the same community. One was almost literally gathered up by the congregation of the church he attended. They lifted him into close communion and fellowship, and his Christian life blossomed. The other was tolerated at the church he chose to attend, but that was all. Though he had made a profession of faith in Christ, the congregation withheld themselves from him. The first of these young men was triumphantly victorious over alcohol addiction; the other failed miserably.

Our churches need to realize that they can perform a vital service for God and their communities by coming to grips with the problem of alcoholism. Alcoholics are all around us. If the churches become concerned and informed about the problem so that they take an intelligent, realistic approach to it, they will soon find that local agencies dealing with the problem on the secular level will be anxious to have the assistance of the church.

It would be good for the pastor and as many lay workers as possible to attend seminars on the subject held by medical schools and psychiatric institutes, also to get acquainted with the men on the staffs of local rescue missions and become involved in their programs.

To be sure, only 3 to 12 percent of the nation's alcoholics wind up on skid row, but they are the most severe cases, and dealing with them will provide very good training in learning how to work with the alcoholic and how fellowship can best be offered to him. Usually the local mission super-intendent will be happy to come and speak to any of the groups in the churches of the community. His concern for the alcoholic should strike a responsive note in the hearts of the church people.

Church libraries ought to have a section with books on the subject of alcohol and alcohol addiction. Such an assortment of books will provide for congregations vital information on a perplexing subject, and especially for those among the congregation who have an alcoholic in their families.

Not only that, but an alcohol addict who sees such books in the church library or sees them mentioned from time to time in the bulletin will realize that the church people are concerned about individuals like him. He might find real help in the books, but even though he didn't read them, the very fact that such books are in the church library can help to make the bond of friendship and fellowship with Christian people a bit stronger.

I would suggest the following books:

Cup of Fury by Upton Sinclair (Great Neck N. Y.: Channel Press, Inc., 1956). This volume will not only give you a view of the problem from the secular standpoint but it will give you some dramatic examples of how the lives of men have been destroyed by drink, and also examples of how others have made a complete recovery from their problem and the methods used. A very excellent book for young people.

Marty Mann's New Primer on Alcoholism by Marty Mann (New York: Holt, Rinehart & Winston, 1958).

How to Help an Alcoholic by Clifford J. Earle (Philadelphia: Westminster Press, 1952). A spiritual approach to the problem.

What Shall We Say About Alcohol? by Caradine R. Hooton (Nashville, Tenn.: Abingdon Press, 1960).

Helping the Alcoholic and His Family by Dr. Thomas Shipp (Englewood Cliffs, N. J.: Prentice-Hall, Inc., 1963).

Out of the Liquid Jungle by Faith Coxe Bailey (Chicago: Moody Press, 1958). Case histories of people who have recovered from the problem of alcoholism through the power of the gospel of the Lord Jesus Christ.

The Disease Concept of Alcoholism by E. M. Jellinek (New Brunswick, N. J.: Hillhouse Press, 1960).

As we consider the church's role in helping the alcoholic, we must not forget that the average alcoholic feels most uncomfortable when he first starts going to church. "They'd fall over in a faint if *I* went to church," I have had such men tell me.

The first few times they come they feel ill at ease. It is up to the members of the congregation to make every effort to show the individual that they not only welcome him but they are *glad* he came.

A small central Nebraska church caught the vision of reaching such people and did something about it. They weren't thinking solely of helping the alcoholic, but God used their efforts in that way. They were concerned about the number of parents who brought their children to Sunday school but didn't stay themselves. Efforts were made to get them into a Sunday school class, but without success. The pastor finally realized that although his congregation was friendly these parents felt strange in church.

So a class was organized to meet in his home during the

Sunday school hour. Coffee was served and the Bible was studied in an informal atmosphere. No effort was made to contact those with special problems, but of the twenty-five enrolled during the first several months (the class divided in two to keep the groups small) it was discovered that three had definite drinking problems. Two of the three have been able to break their alcohol addiction by the power of the gospel of the Lord Jesus Christ. The third is still being worked with. He doesn't feel out of place in the group; he attends regularly and is honestly seeking help.

We might be able to assist the alcoholic by starting a class like this, or through some other means of showing the stranger that he is welcome in our midst. Warmth and fellowship can make the difference in whether or not we reach the alcoholic for Christ and thus meet his spiritual needs.

As we have said before, it matters not whether the person seeking to help an alcoholic is an exalcoholic or not. So long as the love of Christ burns in our hearts and we have compassion for those who are lost, we can be used of God to help the alcohol addict.

Since dealing with the alcoholic requires so much time, the pastor with a burden for those who are slaves to beverage alcohol would be wise to consider the organization of a team to help him. The team would need to be composed of men and women of unqualified dedication to the Lord, men and women of spiritual maturity who are willing to make very real sacrifices for the cause of Christ.

The pastor would also have to enlist families who would be willing to share their homes with strangers, who would be willing to spend any number of evenings with others whose homes and lives have been battered by the bruising forces of alcoholism. Associating with those who have been undergoing great trials and problems isn't always the most pleasant sort of companionship. And any results would have to be measured, necessarily, in months rather than hours. But a vital contribution can be made by Christians who are willing to make sacrifices.

In addition, the pastor should have a good medical doctor on his team, if one is available in his congregation. If not, he may be able to get the help of a physician in the community. Such a man would be most valuable in giving medical advice and assistance when necessary.

The very existence of such a team would be a proof to the alcoholic that the church sincerely desires to help him.

Although the alcoholic needs fellowship desperately, it is not always easy to get him to attend services at church right away. We must remember that the alcoholic often has a fear of people. This, in addition to shame for his actions, makes it hard for him to face an entire congregation. However, a single member of the team could befriend him and provide him with fellowship by arranging to meet with him for Bible study and prayer (perhaps once a week).

I have seen this done. I know it works.

The team member and his wife could go a step further by making friends with the alcoholic's family. They could share God's love on a family basis. The alcoholic's wife would then have a concerned Christian friend to whom she could turn for counsel and advice, and the alcoholic would begin to feel the dignity of being accepted as an individual. As the friendship develops, an attempt could be made to get the alcoholic's family into Sunday school and into the fellowship of the church, or the other way around.

Of course, the pastor, to be effective in his efforts to help the alcoholic, must keep himself well informed on the subject of alcoholism and keep in touch with the local people who have the same interests. He would do well to keep in close touch with AA through their officers and material, the local rescue missions, (if there are any close by), as well as any centers for the treatment of alcoholics. At the latter he should learn the rules of admittance of an alcoholic; then if he is called upon to help an individual who needs hospitalization, he will be able to advise regarding it. The very fact that the pastor and a number of church members are informed on alcohol and the problems of alcohol addicts will make the alcoholic who is beginning to look for answers more ready to seek our help. The scope and effectiveness of the church will widen as the church members are informed and approachable.

There are two organizations dedicated to the purpose of helping the alcoholic to help himself to sobriety and a useful place in society—Alcoholics Anonymous and Alcoholics Victorious. The latter was founded upon the former.

Dr. William Seath, formerly the Executive Director of the Chicago Christian Industrial League, had long been an admirer of AA and was well acquainted with the splendid job they were doing. However, he felt that such a program would be even more effective if it could be brought into the church and be geared to the needs of those alcoholics who had made a profession of Christ. Through talks with AA leaders, medical doctors, and church leaders, he developed and founded Alcoholics Victorious in February, 1948. Although AA is doing a tremendous piece of work, Alcoholics Victorious is primarily designed to assist the local church in more effectively meeting the needs of alcoholics that look to it for guidance. The two organizations are not in competition, but complement one another.

Alcoholics Victorious* has four steps in its yearlong program of advancement. When the individual joins Alcoholics

*For further information on the organization, write National President, Alcoholics Victorious, 28 S. Sangamon St., Chicago, Illinois 60607.

Victorious he receives a novice card, and is a novice for three months. Then he becomes a pathfinder (for three months), and in a proper ceremony is given a pathfinder's card. At the end of six months of abstinence he is given a victor's card which he carries until he has been in the organization for a year. If he should slip and take a drink at any time during the year, he has to start over once more as a novice. When he has made the first three steps and has abstained for a year he is given a crusader's card and pin.

"It is a big event, I can tell you," one AV member told us proudly, referring to receiving the crusader's card and pin.

Alcoholics Victorious has a short but plainly stated creed:

> 1. I realize that I cannot overcome the drink habit myself. I believe that the power of Jesus Christ is available to help me. I believe that through my acceptance of Him as my personal Saviour I am a new man. II Corinthians 5:17.
>
> 2. Because the presence of God is manifested through continued prayer, I will set aside two periods every day for communion with my heavenly Father. I realize my need for daily living. Psalm 24:1-5.
>
> 3. I recognize my need of Christian fellowship, and will therefore fellowship with Christians. I know that in order to be victorious, I must keep active in the service of Christ, and I will help others through my victory.
>
> 4. I do not partake of any beverage containing alcohol. I know that it is the first drink that does the harm. Therefore I do not drink. I will stay away from places where the temptation to drink might be, and from the companions who might tempt me. I can be victorious because I know that God's strength is sufficient to supply all my needs.

AA, too, had a spiritual beginning.

Bill W., one of the cofounders of the organization, made

his first contact with God at the old Calvary Mission in New York City, which was sponsored by the Calvary Protestant Episcopal Church. Writing of his experience Bill said, "At the meeting, Tex, the leader, told us, 'Only Jesus can save.' Somehow the statement did not jar me. . . . Certain men gave their testimonies. . . . Then came the call. Someone was starting forward. . . . Unaccountably impelled,I started too. . . . I knelt among the penitents."

Bill did not have complete victory over alcohol, and went back to drinking. Finally in desperation, he turned himself in to the hospital. ". . . I still gagged badly at the notion of a power greater than myself. But finally . . . my proud obstinancies were crushed. All at once I found myself crying out, 'If there is a God, let Him show Himself. I am ready to do anything. Anything.' Suddenly the room lit up with a great white light. I was caught up in an ecstasy no words can describe. . . . I thought, *No matter how wrong things seem to be, they're still all right. Things are all right with God and His world.*"

While AA feels that it can best serve as a secular organization, it had a strongly spiritual origin and I believe the twelve steps of AA are based on scriptural principles. From my observation and working with AA members over a period of years, those I have known to be faithfully following the twelve steps and living a new life are those who have come to a personal knowledge of the Lord Jesus Christ.

*The AA Grapevine** is a good magazine for a pastor to place in the hands of the individual who indicates he is interested in finding a way out of his prison of alcohol addiction.

How can we help an alcoholic? By creating around him an atmosphere that would create in him a desire for help. One

*AA Grapevine, Inc., 305 East 45th St., New York 17, New York.

of the most effective ways of doing this is to offer him fellowship in the name of our loving Lord of whom it was said,
"God sent not his Son into the world to condemn the world,
but that the world through him might be saved."

4

LONG-SUFFERING

"THE PATIENCE OF JOB would have been sorely tried by an alcoholic." This statement is found in the booklet *Arresting Alcoholism** and may seem like an exaggeration to some, but not to me or to my family. I put my wife and children through that sort of tribulation. I didn't realize then, as I do now, the agony I caused them.

SETTING OUR SIGHTS—ESTABLISHING OUR FOOTING

"This is a faithful saying, and worthy of all acceptation, that Christ Jesus came into the world to save sinners; of whom I am chief. Howbeit for this cause I obtained mercy, that in me first Jesus Christ might shew forth all longsuffering, for a pattern to them which should hereafter believe on him to life everlasting" (I Timothy 1:15-16).

Like Paul, I was a wicked sinner. When I get to thinking of the things I used to do that disgraced my family and hurt them so terribly, although it was years ago and I know that both God and my family have forgiven me, I am still unable to sleep.

But God saved me and delivered me and my family.

He can do the same for any individual—even the degenerate, filthy alcohol addict—who calls upon His name. Christ shows

*Published by the Christopher D. Smithers Foundation of New York City.

127

His long-suffering to us as a pattern for others to follow in their treatment of sinners. No one needs that pattern more than the one with an alcoholic in the family. We need to have the assurance in our hearts that God is not only interested in our alcoholic but loves him and wants to help him. We also need to be aware of our own relationship to God and the problems He had in bringing us to the place where we could be used of Him.

He knows all about us, our heartaches and trials, our disappointments and our deepest desires. And in His Word He gives us hope and encouragement.

The Psalmist says, "But thou, O Lord, art a God full of compassion, and gracious, longsuffering, and plenteous in mercy and truth" (Psalm 86:15).

Patience and the ability to suffer long are traits of character that are not easily attained. We must ask God to make us patient and long-suffering as we deal with our alcoholic. This applies to everyone who is involved in working with him—members of the immediate family, the pastor or counselor, or concerned friends. We must trust God and believe that He is working, regardless of what we see, hear, or feel. Unwavering confidence and trust in God are imperative if we are going to accomplish two goals in working with our alcoholic:

1. Bringing him to the place, if he is still drinking, where he will request help to overcome his drinking problem

2. Exercising long-suffering and patience, if he has reached the place where he is seeking help, to help him up the road to recovery so he will be an asset to the family, his church and his community.

There is little likelihood that these goals will be achieved overnight, or without severe pain and trials. The way will be hard for us and for the individual we are trying to help. Believe me, I know. I have traveled up that road.

We need to be ever mindful of the fact that our confidence

nd trust must be in God. We must believe that it is His
desire to free our alcoholic from the bonds of addiction and
o give him a new life. We will only be disappointed and
heartbroken if we do not look beyond what we see in the
individual with whom we have been working, to God, who will
give us the strength and patience we need during this very
trying period.

"My brethren, count it all joy when ye fall into divers
temptations; knowing this, that the trying of your faith
worketh patience. But let patience have her perfect work,
that ye may be perfect and entire, wanting nothing" (James
:2-4).

Not long ago a Texan wrote of the simple faith and
courage and patience of his wife during the years he was a
slave to beverage alcohol. "She refused to let me break up
our home," he said, "and she refused to lose faith that one
day God would deliver me from alcohol addiction."

This woman put up with a drunkard husband for fifteen
years, her faith never wavering, before God brought her
husband to a saving knowledge of the Lord Jesus Christ and
set him free from alcoholism. In her loneliness, despite all
the bad reports she got about her husband, she stood strong
and unmovable in her faith. With patients and long-suffering
she waited until God answered her prayers. Just so, He will
answer your prayers if you continue to trust Him and do not
grow weary of waiting.

In ministering to the alcoholic, we can find help for such
ministry by reading the story of the prodigal son found in
Luke 15. There we will learn lessons from the son and from
the father.

LESSONS FROM THE SON

Headstrong and wayward, the prodigal demanded all his
inheritance so he could leave home and do as he pleased

without interference from anyone. Knowing there was nothing he would be able to do or say that would change the young man's mind, his father let him go.

The same mulish determination to go his own way which characterized the prodigal is seen in our alcoholic. He is going to do as he pleases and when he pleases. All of the arguments we throw at him and all the fussing we do isn't going to stop him from drinking at this particular point.

The prodigal spent his inheritance in a long orgy of riotous living, during which he gave not one thought to his parents or the anguish he was causing them. His money did not last indefinitely, however. The day came when he was broke and hungry enough to take the most lowly of jobs, that of herding pigs, in order to get something to eat.

Then something happened.

He got to thinking about the home where he had been raised. Even his father's servants received better treatment than he was now receiving. He saw the folly of his life of sin. He saw that he was spiritually and morally bankrupt. He had reached absolute bottom.

In the same way the alcoholic wakes up in his own particular pig sty—in a rescue mission, in a city jail where he has spent the night after being picked up for intoxication, or maybe in a hotel room, or seated on the edge of his bed at home. But the location is not so important as his coming face to face with himself. He knows that he cannot go on in the way he has been going. He begins to compare what he could have with what he has now. His heart starts to burn within him.

The prodigal decided to go home. He went penitently asking nothing.

When the alcoholic reaches the place where he honestly admits that he has a problem with beverage alcohol and wants help, something can be done for him. That is why it is so important for his family to keep their homelife operating a nearly normal as possible. The atmosphere of the home should be such that it will encourage our alcoholic to want to be a normal member of the family once more.

LESSONS FROM THE FATHER

The father of the prodigal kept the home atmosphere as it was, and when the wayward son returned, he was brought into this home and helped.

Dorothy Cameron Disney wrote about the organization Alateens in her monthly feature, Making Marriage Work, in the October, 1962 issue of the *Ladies Home Journal*. She told of Fred, a skinny fourteen-year-old whose mother worked as a department-store clerk. His father, a part-time accountant, was an alcoholic. Miss Disney quoted the boy as saying, "When I came home the other day, my old man was slumped on the sofa and I knew he had been hitting the bottle again. I didn't say a word, just looked at him and started upstairs. Maybe he read my mind. Anyway, he pulled a table lamp out of its socket and threw it at me. I was used to ducking, so I didn't get hurt." Then he asked the question, "What does a kid do when his dad becomes violent?"

The Alateens advice in situations like that is to get completely out of the way until the alcoholic is well and rational again. They then suggest going to an AA member, a clergyman, a doctor, or a close relative, and asking their help. Alateens explain that an alcoholic is often the most brutal to those he loves the most.

The family of the alcoholic will find some excellent advice in the booklet *To Wives and the Family Afterwards* published by Al-Anon.

> Perhaps your husband will make a fair start on the new basis. But just as things are going beautifully, he dismays you by coming home drunk. You are satisfied that he really wants to get over drinking. You need not

be alarmed, though it is infinitely better that he have no relapse at all.

As has been true with many of the men, it is by no means a bad thing in some cases. Your husband will see at once that he must redouble his spiritual activities if he expects to survive. You need not remind him of his spiritual deficiency. He will know it. Cheer him up. Ask him how you can be still more helpful.

The slightest hint of fear or intolerance may lessen your husband's chance of recovery. In a weak moment he may take your dislike of his highstepping friends as one of those insanely trivial excuses to drink. We never, never try to arrange a man's life so as to shield him from temptation. The slightest disposition on our part to guide his appointments or his affairs so he will not be tempted will be noticed. Make him feel absolutely free to come and go as he likes.

If he gets drunk, don't blame yourself. God has either removed your husband's liquor problem or He has not. If not, then it had better be found out right away. Then you and your husband can get down to fundamentals. If a repetition is to be prevented, place the problem, along with everything else, in God's hands.

We have an obligation to run our homes as nearly normal as possible, looking forward to the day when our alcoholic will want to turn from the bottle. When that happens, a normal, smoothly functioning home will provide more help for him than anything else we can do.

Aside from having a well-run home for the prodigal to return to, the father expected an answer to his prayers. He was watching for his boy's return. "But when he was yet a great way off, his father saw him, and had compassion, and ran, and fell on his neck and kissed him" (Luke 15:21).

This is the sort of attitude we must have. After praying, we must expect God to do something in answer to our prayers.

When the son got home, his father let him resume his position in the family, but in the case of the alcoholic this is not so simple as it would seem. We are often surprised to find that serious problems can arise in receiving the alcoholic back into the family. Many times a wife is bitterly disappointed when she discovers that she cannot turn the clock back to the way things were before they were married. We must start where the situation is at the moment, which means that we are going to have to forgive and forget. Forgiving may be easy. It is the forgetting that is hard.

Recovery must start when an alcoholic comes home, honestly wanting to quit drinking. Of course, his own willpower is not enough. He must have Christ as his Saviour so he can have a strong spiritual basis upon which to build. We must build upon this foundation together, growing spiritually and closer to one another.

It may not be easy for us to have in our hearts the joy the prodigal's father had as his son came home and back into the fellowship of the family. This father said, ". . .this my son was dead, and is alive again. He was lost, and is found. And they began to be merry" (Luke 15:24).

A merry, joyful, happy heart will go a long way in helping your alcoholic to a successful recovery. But such a joy can be ours only as a fruit of the Holy Spirit. "The fruit of the Spirit is love, joy, . . ." (Galatians 5:22).

LESSONS FROM THE ELDER SON

The prodigal's father was overjoyed at the fact that his wayward son was home once more, but the elder son in the family was not at all happy about it. He had stayed home and worked dutifully while his younger brother was away from home squandering his share of the family inheritance. He had seen the hurt in his parents' faces and had been touched with jealousy as he saw how they watched the road for sign of the prodigal's return. Now that he was back, the elder brother's jealousy became a consuming fire. You can almost hear him saying, "It isn't fair! It isn't fair at all!"

Although we may not be aware of it, each of us has something of the elder brother's attitude. But if we are going to have the patience and long-suffering needed to help our alcoholic, we are going to have to protect ourselves, and him, from the angry jealousy that will flare every time we think things aren't going just the way we feel they should on this road to recovery.

We have been praying earnestly for the deliverance of our alcoholic from the power of beverage alcohol. We have seen him make a profession of taking Christ as his Saviour and have been happier about that than anything else in the world. Yet, the hurts and heartaches we have suffered are still very personal and real.

We have seen the children suffer. Indeed, it is likely that they are still suffering. We see it in their personalities and in the way we have to live because of the financial situation our alcoholic's drinking has created. If we aren't very careful and aren't living very close to God, we will build such a spirit of resentment that we will explode when things aren't going the way we think they should.

What in the attitude of the elder brother are we going to have to guard against?

First, we will have to guard against jealousy.

I mentioned this on one occasion to a person with whom I was counseling, and she was very much disturbed.

"What do you mean, jealousy?" she bristled. "I've been longing and praying for years that my husband would be set free from the hold liquor has on him. How can you say that I could ever be jealous of him if that should happen?"

I went on to tell her of a woman who was in exactly the same position and how jealous she got without even realizing it. She was jealous of her place in the hearts and lives of their children. During the years her husband was drinking so heavily, the children came to her for advice and counsel. She was the one who enforced discipline. She was the focal point in their lives.

Suddenly her alcoholic husband was sober. He took an interest in the children, and they began to come to him with decisions instead of to their mother. As he assumed his rightful position in the home, she was filled with resentment and became irritable, angry, and very jealous. Her jealousy was such an important factor that it almost caused her husband to be defeated in his fight for sobriety. Fortunately she was wise enough to see what had happened to her, once it was pointed out, and she did something about it.

Even having our alcoholic accepted back into the community once more can create jealousy which Satan can use as a barb against him. If he is making a successful recovery, he wants to tell somebody else about it. We may think he gets a bit too involved in church activities, or in making his 12-step calls for Alcoholics Anonymous, or in his responsibilities in Alcoholics Victorious. It is very easy for us to feel neglected and abused.

"I used to be a 'bottle widow,' " one lovely Christian wife told me. "But now, I guess you'd have to say I'm some other kind of a widow. My husband is always giving his testimony in some church or going somewhere to witness to someone."

In her case, however, she was mature enough in her Christian experience to understand and accept it.

"But I don't care," she continued. "As long as he's not drinking and is trying to lead someone else to Christ, I'm happy."

The second trait of the elder son that we must guard against is self-pity.

"Lo, these many years do I serve thee, neither transgressed

I at any time thy commandment: and yet thou never gavest
me a kid, that I might make merry with my friends" (Luke
15:29).

Self-pity is apt to rear its ugly head and blight our lives if
we don't recognize it and pray for victory over it.

Many average alcohol addicts have staggering financial
problems. Their wives have had to work to support the
family and to maintain some kind of economic stability. Suppose, in a situation such as this, the alcoholic makes a
financial investment without mentioning it to his wife and
loses all the money—money that is so desperately needed.
There is a very real danger in such a case that the wife might
feel so abused and resentful that her attitude, even though
she says little, might drive her husband back to drinking
again.

Or take the husband of an alcoholic wife as an example.
She has been making good progress for some time. The
routine of the home is almost back to normal. Rejoicing
that they are going to have a normal life again, the husband
asks his boss out to dinner.

The wife doesn't drink, but she's so nervous and upset that
she can't manage everything. The meat is burned and the
dinner is a miserable failure. I've heard husbands in situations like that air their feelings bitterly.

"I've put up with this sort of thing for years," they say.
"I've tried to be a good husband and provide a good house
and furniture and all that goes with it, but even when she's
sober she isn't a good housekeeper."

To keep from pitying ourselves and allowing self-pity to
destroy the progress that has been made, we must patiently
wait upon the Lord and show long-suffering to the alcoholic.

The third fault of the elder brother is the way he constantly remembered the past.

He forgave nothing and forgot nothing. He held against

his brother everything that had happened. "But as soon as this thy son was come, which hath devoured thy living with harlots, thou hast killed for him the fatted calf" (Luke 15: 30).

We, too, find it difficult to put away all that happened in the past. We profess to forget, but we don't, really. We keep looking at our alcoholic and at everything he does.

"That's just the way he used to do before he went on a drunk," we say, fearfully measuring his every action.

If we are going to be able to help our alcoholic, what shall we do with our memories of the way things used to be? We've got to face things as they are now and build solidly from the point where we now stand.

In spite of the danger of allowing the traits of the elder brother to crop out in our lives and cause untold mischief, there is a way of victory. The prodigal's father took this way of victory. He said to the elder brother, "It was meet that we should make merry, and be glad: for this thy brother was dead, and is alive again; and was lost, and is found" (Luke 15:32).

We must constantly remind ourselves that our alcoholic is like that prodigal son. Once he was lost. Now he is found. Once he was dead. Now he lives. If we want to be successful in helping our alcohol addict along the road to recovery, we must combine praise for good things with our long-suffering and patience. And you can be long-suffering and patient if you have the confidence and trust expressed by the Psalmist David when he wrote: "In thee, O LORD, do I put my trust; . . . For thou art my rock and my fortress; therefore for thy name's sake lead me, and guide me. . . . Into thy hand I commit my spirit: thou hast redeemed me, O LORD God of truth. . . . Oh how great is thy goodness, which thou hast laid up for them that fear thee; which thou hast wrought for them that trust in thee before the sons of men! Thou shalt hide them in the secret of thy presence from the pride of man: thou shalt keep them secretly in a pavilion from the strife of tongues. . . . Be of good courage, and he shall strengthen your heart, all ye that hope in the Lord" (Psalm 31:1, 3, 5, 19-20, 24).

5

FIRMNESS

SOMEWHERE, SOMEHOW, we have gotten the misconceived idea that there is no rebuke in God's love; that it is sickeningly sweet and forgiving, even though we are unrepentant and our sin is unconfessed. We act as though we believe that because God loves so much He would never punish anyone. This is not true.

God loves us so much He will not allow us to name Christ as Saviour and continue in our old sin without severely chastising us to bring us back to Him.

LET THE ALCOHOLIC STAND ON HIS OWN TWO FEET

Christ gave explicit instructions to the disciples how they should act in the face of sin and wrongdoing: "Take heed to yourselves: If thy brother trespass against thee, rebuke him; and if he repent, forgive him. And if he trespass against thee seven times in a day, and seven times in a day turn again to thee, saying, I repent; thou shalt forgive him" (Luke 17: 3-4).

If we sin, we should be rebuked. If we repent, we ought to be forgiven. This is the way Christ says that we should do with one another. God does the same in His relationships with us. Because He loves us He cannot allow us to sin without rebuking us.

". . . rebuke a wise man, and he will love thee" (Proverbs 9:8).

"Let the righteous smite me; it shall be a kindness: and let him reprove me; for it shall be an excellent oil, which shall not break my head: for yet my prayers also shall be in their calamities" (Psalm 141:5).

And when we deal with the alcohol addict, we shall need to rebuke him, for in his downward progression into alcoholism he has developed three characteristics:

1. He has become a crafty liar.
2. He seeks someone to lean upon and becomes a very dependent individual.
3. He thinks only of himself and much prefers to be alone. His personality becomes egocentric and antisocial.

If our alcoholic is going to be helped, not only must his addiction to beverage alcohol be broken, his very personality is going to have to be redeveloped. If our alcoholic lies to us, we should quietly but firmly let him know that we know he is lying. The sooner he comes to the place where he has to face the truth, the sooner he is going to be set free from his warped personality and his addiction to beverage alcohol.

The pamphlet, *Trial and Error*, published by the Alcohol and Drug Addiction Research Foundation of Ontario, Canada, brings out the same thought in its instructions for those who have an alcoholic in the family: "The average alcoholic would not be able to function as long as he does if his wife or mother would allow him to stand on his own two feet where he properly belongs. Let him accept responsibility for his own actions. Allow him to retain his self-respect instead of slowly helping him to destroy himself."

MAKE GROUND RULES

It is not wise to threaten the alcoholic. Neither is it a good practice to try to extract promises from him. But if our alcoholic should voluntarily make a promise when he is sober, he should be held to his agreement.

A couple who faced a situation of this sort came to me some time ago and asked me to marry them. Although they were both in their fifties, neither had been married before. Moreover, the man was an alcohol addict who had been dry for only six months. I knew him well since I had been counseling with him for three years.

"Sally has wanted to marry you for five years," I reminded him, "but she has refused because of your drinking. If you are going to get married there has to be an agreement that you will not drink."

He nodded readily.

"If you take so much as a thimbleful of liquor, you should be put out of the house."

Both of them agreed that this was the only basis upon which they could have a happy marriage.

They had been married nine months when Tom took a glass of wine.

Tearfully she asked me over the phone, "What should I do now?"

"You know what the agreement was," I reminded her.

She packed his clothes and put him out of the house. "When you're through drinking and ready to try to live a sober life again, you can come back," she said. "But not before."

She threw him out of the house ten different times in two and a half years before he finally yielded to the Lord.

"I was lying on a hospital bed alone," he said, "when I realized that there was only one way I could be free. So I said, 'God, you take my life.'"

Today he has been completely delivered from addiction, and there is joy in that home because a wife stood firm. It wasn't easy for her. We spent much time in counseling her and helping her through those difficult periods. But the result was victory through Christ. You, too, can have such a victory, if you remain firm.

PROTECT YOUR INTERESTS

Rev. Joseph Kellerman, Director of the Charlotte, North Carolina Council on Alcoholism, gives another warning. "Don't let the alcoholic outsmart you, for this teaches him to avoid responsibility and lose respect for you at the same time. Don't let the alcoholic exploit you or take advantage of you, for in so doing you'll become an accomplice in the evasion of responsibility."

I will never forget a couple that came to me with this sort of a problem. The wife had a sizable bank account when they were married. Her husband insisted that she transfer her assets into a joint account, which she refused to do. When they came to me in a normal marriage counseling session to talk about the matter, it soon was brought out that he had a serious drinking problem. She had thought he would quit when they were married, but he hadn't.

As the session went on, it was apparent that he had insisted on seeing a counselor because he hoped he would find someone who would agree with him that her money should be in a joint account.

"You know," I said to him privately, "I'm talking to you as one old drunk to another. When I was drinking I used to do anything and everything I could to outsmart my employers and my wife in order to get more time and more money to do my drinking. Are you sure this isn't why you want your wife's money in a joint account?"

He admitted that it was, and we were able to help him see his responsibility and to assume it.

MEAN WHAT YOU SAY

It is not wise to make threats to our alcoholic, but if we do, we must make sure we're prepared to carry them out.

The woman who said she had threatened to leave her husband a hundred times for his drinking finally did so. It wasn't long until he was seeking help so he could get her back.

At the Open Door Mission we make no threats to the men in our rehabilitation program, but we have some very definite regulations. The men know when they come into our program voluntarily that if they have so much as a single beer, they will be removed from the program. If they want to come back in, they must start at the bottom and work their way up once more.

Usually the men have trouble in the second month of the program. That is when they are permitted to go out and work several days a week and keep the money. If they take a drink, we make them pack their clothes and leave. Some come back and try again. The second time they are usually successful.

What works with the men at the Mission will work with our alcoholic. We must be firm and mean what we say.

DON'T DO FOR HIM WHAT HE SHOULD DO

Women often have to go to work to support themselves and their families because of the alcohol addiction of their husbands. Out of necessity they begin to assume the full responsibility of the home and require nothing of their husbands.

It isn't easy for our alcoholic to get a job or hold one. He has probably spent a long period of time drifting from one job to another or not working at all. He has forgotten what it is like to have to work every day. However, he should be willing to assume some responsibility for the support and upkeep of his home.

In his moments of sobriety share with him the needs of the home, not as a nagging wife but as a loving wife who still believes that the husband is the head of the house. Impress upon him that he should share and give advice in those areas of responsibility.

When he starts working again, don't hold onto your job for reasons of security—because you feel he might have a relapse. If you feel you must keep your job, arrange to live on his salary. Discuss the matter with him and reach an agreement so he will never get the idea that he can fall back on you to take care of things. Work things out so he will always feel his responsibility.

There is a very good chance, if this dependence is not broken, that he might go back to drinking again.

One of the benefits of presenting the gospel to the alcohol addict is that his faith in God will enable him to transfer his dependency from an individual or a group to God. God is the only one who can really help him and supply the strength and wisdom he needs in order to assume his responsibility. When an individual begins to assume responsibility, it isn't long until he begins to regain his self-respect. Another benefit from his faith in God is that his faith removes the tendency toward self-destruction, a tendency which is common to the alcoholic.

ASK ADVICE

Those who deal with a known alcoholic should always get advice from outside sources when a problem arises within the family. For instance, some time ago, a lovely Christian mother whose heart was being broken by the drinking of her alcoholic son called us for advice. Her son had been a very successful broker. Few people aside from his business

partners, his closest friends and his family—a prominent
family in our city—even knew that he had a drinking problem.
His partners in the brokerage firm kept him on at full salary
for a number of years. Finally, when the situation got so
bad they could no longer put up with it, they relieved him
of all responsibility, but placed him on a pension. His wife
drank herself to death and he seemed bent on doing the same
thing.

It was at this point that his mother, thinking she might be
able to help him, took him into her home. She was financially
independent, but an unmarried daughter lived with her.
The daughter had a job, contributed to the upkeep of the
home and gave her mother the fellowship and companionship
she needed. When the son moved in, nothing was said to
him about his responsibilities. He moved into a room and
proceeded to drink as much as before. The only thing that
changed was the location.

When the situation became more than the two women
could bear, they called me. When I arrived at their home, I
found he had been in a drunken stupor for days. We got him
to the hospital where he was dried out and released.

I tried to talk with him, but he would not listen.

When I talked with his mother and sister, I explained that
he should have to pay his way, make some contribution to the
expenses of the family, and should also participate in the
family life and fellowship—that he should not just stay in
his room. I tried to make them see that they had to break
his dependency.

They didn't accept my advice. They didn't understand
the problem, and they thought the requirements I set down
were too hard, and not loving enough.

It wasn't long until I was called once more and asked to
get him into the hospital. "No," I told them, "I'll not take
him to the hospital this time. I suggest that you make a

committal and have the authorities place him in the psychiatric ward of the County Hospital."

They didn't think this was very kind, either, but they did it.

The shock of having a deputy sheriff take him to the County Hospital was just what he needed to wake him up to the fact that he had a problem and had to have some help. When he got home, he was ready for guidance. Some ground rules were laid down as to his responsibilities toward his family. He assumed them, and today he is a help to his mother rather than a liability, and all because she sought advice and followed it.

Actions Speak Louder Than Words

In working with an alcoholic we must always go by what he does—not by what he says he is going to do. We should pay attention to what he says so we can help him hold to it, but we have to watch his actions to see if he is living up to what he says.

I often talk with men who start to drinking again after they have been dry for as long as a year or more. Usually they are horrified to find that they have again plummeted to the very depths of drunkenness.

I always go to great lengths to explain to them once more this terrible problem of addiction. This is something about which we must constantly remind our alcoholic, since many such people have an idea in the back of their minds that they are going to make a successful recovery from alcoholism and then go back to drinking socially once more. We must always direct our activities with our alcoholic in such a way that we do not encourage social drinking.

Often, when I am talking with a man who has started to drink again after having been sober for a period, he will express bewilderment at what happened. "I can't understand it," he will say. "I want my family back worse than anything else in the world. I don't know why I would do what I did."

Sometimes an alcoholic can't understand why his family won't take him back immediately, and then we must point out to our alcoholic the areas where he is failing. For example, he must understand that just the matter of going back to drink is something that is going to retard the reconciliation for three or six months—possibly another year. No wife in her right mind is going to want to go back into the same old routine that caused all the trouble.

Then, too, it might be that he hasn't been doing anything constructive in trying to redeem his family. Perhaps he isn't making any contribution to their upkeep other than what has been required of him in a court order. He may not make any effort to find out how he can help his wife and children over and above this requirement in assuming his responsibilities as a husband and father.

He may say he wants his family back, but he gives the lie to what he says by making no effort to do those things he knows would show his wife that he is a different person.

One fellow I have been dealing with would take his children to Sunday school but would never go to church himself. He claims to be making a recovery from alcohol addiction. He attends AA meetings once a week and claims that he is getting the spiritual backing he needs. Yet his wife doesn't see him going to church, and she knows that his habits haven't changed. He might not be drinking, but he is still hanging around the same old haunts with the same old friends.

He can talk about being different, but his actions reveal that he is the same fellow he has always been. The only difference is that he hasn't had a drink. However, that doesn't keep his wife from thinking that he is going to start drinking again. And, of course, when he does fall over the line into another bout of drunkenness, she is sure to feel there is no hope for him, or that it will be a long time before she can even think about taking him back.

There are the things we need to watch intelligently in our alcoholic. We need to be sure that his actions are where his desires and his talk are. When his actions change, we can be quite sure that he is changed, too.

Every once in a while we come across some refreshing experiences. One such occasion was when my wife and I traveled some distance from Omaha to speak to an AA group. We met a local politician there who had not been married long although both he and his wife were in their late fifties. Strangely enough, neither one had been married before.

My wife learned, as she talked with the wife, the reason for their late marriage. "We went together for sixteen years," she said, "but I wouldn't marry him because I knew he had a drinking problem. When he was delivered from his addiction by the power of God, I agreed to marry him. That was five years ago."

That is the sort of firmness we must have in dealing with an alcoholic.

I came across just the opposite type of woman in dealing with a couple who have since left Omaha. The wife talked as though she wanted her husband to be free from addiction, but I noticed that she seemed to get enjoyment from the fact that he was an alcoholic. One day as I was seated in their home, I learned what the problem was when she said, "I just can't understand why Joe is like he is. I try to be kind to him, and as considerate as I can be. Why, I even bring breakfast to him in bed every morning."

In later counseling sessions I began to point out to her that she wasn't really interested in seeing her husband escape his addiction, that she was interested in being a mother to him. We helped her to see that God's plan is for the husband to be the head of the wife and as a father exercise authority over his children.

She saw that what I said was true, and she was able to face up to her attitude and come to the place where she was willing to change her attitude by the power of God. Then she was able to make a real contribution to our efforts to help her husband make a successful recovery.

BREAKING COMMUNITY DEPENDENCE

Earlier in the chapter we mentioned the problem of the alcoholic becoming dependent upon the community. Every city and town in America faces this problem.

For example, one city with which I am familiar is spending two million dollars a year in an attempt to cure 285 individuals of alcohol addiction. A look at the case histories of these men will reveal the startling fact that most of them rotate from one institution to another, year after year, without being helped. They depend upon community institutions for their survival and for aid and support.

At the Open Door Mission we continually try to break the alcoholic's dependence on the community. It is not easy. We have found that it requires very close community cooperation to make any progress at all in breaking such dependence.

In dealing with this matter on a community level we have found that we are dealing with three types of alcoholic individuals.

1. *The institutionalized alcoholic.*

He has lived in an institution most of his life. He may have worked as a gandy dancer on the railroad, or in construction crews where he has lived in dormitories and eaten in cafeterias or chow lines. Perhaps he has spent long periods of his life in some jail or penitentiary or—because of his addiction—in a hospital for the treatment of alcoholism. At any rate, he becomes so accustomed to the care and routine of an institution that it is difficult for him to live outside such an atmosphere. When he does live outside an institution, he goes back to drink.

We need to recognize this man's problem and help him to regain his self-respect. Working toward this end, we must furnish him with the right kind of atmosphere in which to live. He needs a home in a county institution (not a jail or mental hospital) where he can receive board and room, laundry, and a small salary. He could be used to clean public buildings or to care for the lawns and parks that belong to the county or city. His work should be the kind that will make a contribution to society. Providing a social situation like this will help him to overcome his alcohol addiction, and he will be paying his own way, thus saving the community and taxpayers the expense of caring for him.

2. *The probationary alcoholic.*

Probationary alcoholics are by far the largest group of alcoholics and are men who will need many counseling sessions. Some will require hospitalization to help them make a recovery, but they will need more than hospitalization to be successfully rehabilitated. After they have been dried out, someone is going to have to work with them for a long while, guiding and counseling them.

Most of these men could be productive. They are skilled or semiskilled laborers and could assume the responsibility of taking care of their families, who may be on ADC or some other kind of government relief.

It seems to me that a program should be worked out which will permit such men to live in the institutions where they are committed (men of this type usually come into our institutions through the courts because of drunkenness), and

spend their nights there but could spend the day working
on normal jobs. Their wages could be sent to the family for
support so they could be removed from the relief rolls.

This would do two things. First, it would help break the
dependency of this individual on the community for the
support of his family. Second, not many men would care to
continue in an arrangement where they had to spend their
time in an institution and still had to work to support their
families. My experience with the treatment of alcoholics
leads me to the conviction that it wouldn't be long until such
men would be looking for some type of an intelligent program
to help them get over their alcohol addiction.

While a program of this type would have some legal com-
plications, they should not be insurmountable.

Most alcoholics are good workmen, and it should not be
difficult to induce employers to cooperate with such a program. Such a program would also give an opportunity for
cooperation between the community, the employer and the
family in an effort to help this man to overcome his problem
and to return to society as a useful citizen.

3. *The rehabilitated alcoholic.*

This is the individual who came for help, went through
the program of rehabilitation, received what was offered to
him gratefully, and has put it to use. He is restored to his
family and is finding his place in his church and the community.

What a joy it is to see such results in an individual who was
an alcoholic!

God can make our alcoholic into that type of person. We
can cooperate with God by praying for our alcoholic, presenting the gospel to him, offering him fellowship, being patient

and long-suffering, and being firm. It will not be easy. It may take a long while, but we can rest in the assurance that God will do what He has promised.

Keep looking up. He will bless us just as much as we will let Him!

Part III

FIVE WAYS THE ALCOHOLIC CAN HELP HIMSELF

INTRODUCTION

I AM AN ALCOHOLIC.

I know what it is like to burn with a desire to drink that is so overpowering that family, jobs, and friends mean nothing compared to the desire for liquor. I know what it is like to wake up in a hotel room not knowing where I was or how I got there.

I also know the joy of complete deliverance from the power of alcohol addiction and never cease to praise God for such deliverance.

The first two sections of this book have been written to help pastors, counselors, and the families of alcoholics to understand people like me—and you.

If you have a drinking problem, this section is directed especially to you.

I hope you have carefully read what has gone before. I hope you have studied the chapters on the alcoholic personality and the cycle. Whether you want to admit it or not, we alcoholics are addicted to ethyl alcohol. If you are going to break the hold alcohol has on you, you are going to have to face up to the problem and totally abstain from the use of beverage alcohol for the rest of your life.

When I made the break, I had to have all the help I could get. You, too, are going to need help.

The purpose of this last section of the book is to help you in a very practical way in your struggle to sobriety. The counsel given in these five chapters has been given to hundreds of men in the more than ten years that I have been helping alcoholics. The information has been gleaned from lectures I have given to men who have been making a successful recovery in our New Life Program—men from every stratum of society and every walk of life. I have seen men successfully follow the road to recovery which is outlined in the next five chapters. I know that you too can successfully follow this road to recovery if your desire to be sober and respected in the community is strong enough to motivate you to turn your life completely over to God.

1

TRANSFER HIS DEPENDENCY TO GOD

"I DON'T UNDERSTAND MYSELF at all, for I really want to do what is right, but I can't. I do what I don't want to—what I hate" (Romans 7:15, *Living Letters*).

No one understands the meaning of that verse better than an alcoholic. We want to do what is right. Oh, how we want to be restored to our families and to become respected members of the community once more! However, our craving for beverage alcohol is so powerful we cannot overcome it. You would have to search the world to find a person who has more feelings of guilt and remorse, or feels any more sorry for himself, than alcoholics do. In the throes of our addiction we are, of all men, most miserable.

And not without reason.

We realize, with vague uneasiness, that our personalities are breaking down. We know our ability to do our work is slipping from us. Our families are drifting away or are already gone, and our friends leave us.

We're caught up in a terrifying wheel within a wheel. We are trying to make a recovery and at the same time to satisfy our craving for beverage alcohol. We experience one failure after another. Time and again we make a firm decision to leave liquor alone, followed by a terrible, losing battle and a

miserable sickening drunk that triggers another, and another
and another. At last, we come to the place where we feel there
is no hope for us. And we give ourselves over to the misery
of eking out an existence from one bottle to another.

We become strangers to our loved ones and even to ourselves. To get another bottle, we lie and cheat and steal with
animal cunning in an effort to outsmart those who are trying
to help us. We will make miserable exhibitions of ourselves
before anyone who happens to be around, yet we are too
proud to admit that we have a problem with alcohol. We
hate what we are and long for help, yet we are too self-centered
to ask for it. We would give anything we own to get our
family back, yet we're too proud to make any attempt to win
them. Added to all these thoughts is the nagging thought
that nobody loves us. In fact, we even begin to lose any love
we had for ourselves.

To such a person—feeling so unloved—the message that God
loves him comes as good news. God's love is a mystery no
one can completely understand, but I know its reality! I
myself have experienced this love of God, which we read
about in His Word: "But God showed His great love for us
by sending Christ to die for us while we were still sinners"
(Romans 5:8, *Living Letters*).

As an inmate in one of the Texas prisons in 1948 after a
two-year drunk that landed me there, I hit bottom. I began
to look for a way to straighten out my life and discovered
Christ as the answer. I was led to this discovery when I read
the title of a tract on the chaplain's reading table: *Why Not
Try God?*

"Why not try God?" I asked myself. "You've tried everything else." And I had.

Then I took the geographical cure. I thought I could run
from liquor, but I wound up on skid row. I tried a tour in
the army, thinking that would change me. It didn't help a

bit. I made a comeback of sorts after my discharge, but began to slip again, so I tried psychiatry. I still drank as much as ever. I even tried the church, if you can call sitting in a service once a week as trying the church. As another alcoholic, you already know why none of those things worked with me. I wouldn't *let* them work.

The title of that tract still gnawed at me, and when I got back to my cell I began to read the Bible the Gideons had placed there some five years before. It was then that I made the discovery that God is holy. "There is none holy as the LORD: . . . neither is there any rock like our God" (I Sam. 2: 2).

From my days in Sunday school and what I read in the Bible I understood that sin cut one off from God. Then I made another startling discovery. I had a sinful nature. This is well expressed in Romans 8:17, *Living Letters*: "I know I am rotten through and through so far as my old sinful nature is concerned. No matter which way I turn I can't make myself do right. I want to but I can't."

Up until this time, I had supposed that I was a sinner because of the wicked things I had done. Then I made the startling discovery that because of my sinful nature I, Jerry Dunn, had drifted into alcohol addiction, had left my wife and family, and was a liar and a cheat.

I felt the way the Apostle Paul must have felt when he wrote, "So you see how it is: my new life tells me to do right, but the old nature that is still inside me loves to sin. Oh, what a terrible thing this is! Who will free me from this slavery to this deadly lower nature?" (Romans 7:24-25, *Living Letters*).

God was holy! I was sinful! How could I ever be delivered from my sinful nature?

At Christmas time the same year, as I read the Christmas story I read this verse: "And she shall bring forth a son, and

thou shalt call his name JESUS: for he shall save his people
from their sin" (Matthew 1:21).

The thought fascinated me. If Jesus Christ came to be a
Saviour, I wanted to find out how He could save me. So I
began to study the life of Christ. As I searched the Scriptures,
I learned that Christ came to give life. "So whosoever has
God's Son, has life; whosoever does not have His Son, does
not have life" (I John 4:12, *Living Letters*). Jesus Christ
said of Himself, "I am come that they might have life, and
that they might have it more abundantly" (John 10:10).

I couldn't understand what the Bible said about being
dead in trespasses and sin, but it wasn't very hard for me to
look at my past and to know that I hadn't been really living,
that my entire life was a continual search for something that
I had been missing. Spiritually, I was dead.

Everywhere I looked in those days I saw dead men whose
lives had been wasted away. I thought of a lot of my old drinking buddies. Most of them hadn't gone as deep into sin as I
had, but they were just as dead as I was. They were searching
for satisfaction and direction for their lives. They longed to
have purpose and be alive.

I knew I was dead and the thing that I needed was life.
My heart cried out for life, but I was so unfamiliar with the
Scriptures that I didn't know there was a Bible verse that
would have answered the cry of my heart: "For whosoever
shall call upon the name of the Lord shall be saved" (Romans
10:13).

But that day in my cell I knew I had reached the end of
the road as far as I was concerned. I cried out in my heart, "I
need a new life! Jesus, you said that you came to give a new
life. You said that it would be an abundant life. That's what
I need. That's what I want. That's what I take!"

I didn't know anything about theology. I didn't really
know anything about the death and resurrection of our Lord

Jesus Christ, except what I had heard since I was a small child. All I was really sure of was that I had a need, and deep down inside of me I knew that Jesus Christ was the answer to that need. I asked Him to fill my need. He did. It was as simple as that.

I was surprised to discover, when I began to consider what I had done, that I had entered into a transaction with God. Somehow I knew that from that day forward I was never going to be the same guy.

God hadn't made any demands of me. He hadn't told me to prove myself when I got out of the penitentiary and go to church and then He would hear me. He didn't even tell me to stop drinking. At that time I didn't have any idea whether I could ever stop drinking or not. He was there when I needed Him and came to Him in honesty, asking for a new life.

He will do the same for you.

The next few weeks were exciting ones as I discovered new and wonderful things in the Word of God. For instance, I read in II Corinthians 5:17 (*Living Letters*), "When someone becomes a Christian he becomes a brand new person inside. He is not the same any more. A new life has begun!"

I didn't try to argue with what I read. I didn't try to figure it out. I didn't even try to understand how it could be. I had new life. I was a new creature. All things had become new. And somehow, at that very moment, I knew I was going to be delivered from addiction to alcohol. I knew it because of what God's Word said.

At that time I had to *believe* I had a new life. Now I can look back and see how new and wonderful it *actually* has been.

If you are doubting that such an experience can be yours, doubt no more. In all the years that I have been working with alcoholics I have worked personally with men of all ages and positions in life. Some were rich and some were poor. I have dealt with men who were groveling in the worst and most disgusting of sins. I have dealt with men who were chronic alcoholics for many years. Yet I have never seen a man who has honestly and sincerely confessed his sin and turned his life completely to God who hasn't been delivered from the power of beverage alcohol.

Yes, God was for me. He is for you. God is for the alcoholic.

Transfer Your Dependency to God

In an essay entitled *Drugs That Shape Men's Minds,* Aldous Huxley says, "We love ourselves to the point of idolatry. But we also dislike ourselves. . . . There is in all of us a desire, sometimes latent, sometimes conscious, and passionately expressed, to escape from the prison of our individuality."

Those of us who have been under the domination of beverage alcohol know this is only too true. From social drinking we have gone down into addiction. We have reached the place where we depend on the bottle to escape from ourselves and the messes we have made of our lives. This is a vicious circle that all but destroys us. We need to learn to transfer our dependency from the bottle to God.

That is the first way in which we, as alcoholics, can help ourselves.

We're going to have to recognize that we have been depending upon beverage alcohol and to realize that this dependency must be broken, although we have no power to break it ourselves.

The first step in the twelve steps of AA puts it this way: "To admit that we are powerless over alcohol and that our lives have become unmanageable."

Alcoholics Victorious say it a little differently. "I realize that I cannot overcome the drink habit by myself. I believe that the power of Jesus Christ is available to help me. I believe that, through my acceptance of Him as my personal Saviour, I am a new man."

Our Lord Jesus Christ says, "Come unto me, all ye that labor and are heavy laden, and I will give you rest. Take my yoke upon you, and learn of me; for I am meek and lowly in heart: and ye shall find rest unto your souls. For my yoke is easy, and my burden is light" (Matthew 11:28-30).

There is just one thing that can keep us from transferring our dependency from the bottle to God. *Ourselves.* We love ourselves better than anything or anyone else in the world. To acknowledge that we can no longer manage ourselves is a difficult thing to do.

But once we look at our lives realistically and recognize that only God can give us the power through which we can be delivered, we are in a position where we can be helped. We go to Him to receive that power. Then the transfer will be complete and we will have rest for our souls, as Christ said.

THE NEW LIFE PRINCIPLE

In addition to our reluctance to give up control of our lives, there is another reason why we hesitate to come to Christ and receive a new life. We fear we won't be able to live as a Christian is expected to. We say, "I'd never be able to do all the things I should, so there's no use in trying."

We must remember that spiritual life starts with birth, just as physical life does. Christ said to Nicodemus, "Ye must be born again."

A person will experience the new birth when he reaches the place where he is actually convicted of his sinful state and puts his trust in Christ to save him. Following birth there should be growth. Growth depends on a knowledge of God's Word, which enables us to understand the things of the Lord and how He would have us to live.

It is well to consider carefully the principles of spiritual

birth and growth. They will help us to understand why some
people who have been going to church all their lives still
aren't living the way Christians should.

We must be very careful to tell those with whom we deal
never to look at those who name Christ as Saviour but don't
live up to their profession. Such people either have never
been born again or have never grown spiritually after they
accepted Christ as their Saviour. The failures of such people
will not excuse anyone for not accepting Christ as Saviour.

Every Christian must feed on the Word of God in order
to grow in the Lord. This is especially true of those of us
who are alcoholics. If we would continue to abstain from
drinking, we must stay close to God. We must grow in the
Lord.

Earlier in these pages I mentioned receiving a postcard
that gave me the best advice I ever had: "Spend fifteen
minutes in reading the Word and fifteen minutes in prayer
every morning and you'll grow in grace and the knowledge
of the Lord."

That advice, given to me about three months after I gave
my heart to God, has become the cornerstone of my Christian
life. This same advice is also one of the main cornerstones
of our New Life Program at the Mission. The men who read
their Bibles and spend time daily with the Lord in prayer
grow spiritually. Those who neglect it often fall away from
what they have professed.

The Scriptures say, "Desire the sincere milk of the word."
From this we see that a new Christian is like a baby who needs
a baby formula. A baby needs to be nurtured carefully
through those important first months. Then, too, no one
expects an infant to walk and talk on the first day of his
birth or during his first few months. We expect him to crawl
first, and then learn to walk.

Since the food of a new-born Christian is as important as

the food needed by a new-born baby, we would do well to consider very carefully the diet needed by a new Christian.

When such an individual comes to me for help, I give him this formula: Read the Gospel of John through very carefully and slowly, a chapter or two each day. Let God speak through the words.

"What you don't understand," I explain, "lay aside, and go on. When you have read the Book of John through once, go back and read it again and again until you have read it five times. When you read it the last time, take a red pencil and underline the word 'believe' whenever you come to it."

It will help to remember that the Greek word for "believe" means literally "to cleave to, to trust, to have faith in, to rely on."

When a new convert has finished the Gospel of John, I urge him to read the Book of Romans in the same way. Then I tell him, "The last time you read it, look up all the cross references. Looking up the references will take you into practically every part of the Bible. You will begin to see the difference between the Old and New Testaments and how one complements the other." This is a slow, painstaking process, but once the new Christian has finished it, he will be ready to follow a program of regular Bible study.

We urge such an individual to seek the help of his pastor or spiritual counselor in setting up a regular Bible study program. As the new convert feeds on God's Word daily, he will be surprised at the joy he will find in using the Bible instead of the bottle as an answer to his problems. He will find that as he grows in his knowledge of God his faith is growing, and so he comes to depend on God more completely.

Here is something for the alcoholic to remember always. God loves him and wants to give him life—life eternal, which starts immediately, as soon as he receives Christ as his Saviour.

2

TALK WITH GOD DAILY

SPEAK OF PRAYER, and the chances are that the
hearer will get a mental picture of a fancy, polished, semi-
formal address to God, or a few rhyming lines learned as a
child. We tend to make prayer too difficult and complex; we
think only persons with a good education and a ready com-
mand of flowery language can pray. We forget that prayer is
simply talking with God, and that God listens when we call
upon Him.

"The Lord is nigh unto all them that call upon him, to all
that call upon him in truth. He will fulfill the desire of them
tha fear him: he also will hear their cry, and will save him"
(Psalm 145:18-19).

If we have a personal relationship with God—if we know
Him through belief of the truth of the gospel of Christ, we
can know that we are never alone. At any time of the day or
night we can call on Him, and He will hear us and answer
our cry for help in trouble or temptation. And it's well to
remember that temptation comes to everyone.

A friend of mine who is separated from his wife is trying
to make a recovery. He longs to have her and his children
back with him again, but the road to recovery is rugged. On
the day we were talking he had called his wife and invited her

out for the evening. "Oh, I don't think I'd better go," she said coyly, "I've already turned down one phone call this evening."

A fit of jealousy seized him, and later, talking to me, he said, "Jerry, would you believe me if I told you I was tempted to go out and get a drink?"

"Sure, I believe you," I answered.

Everybody has temptations. They come when we're not feeling our best or when we are irritated or disturbed about something. The temptation that comes to alcoholics is the burning desire to take another drink; to go back to the bottle and forget this rough road to recovery.

What does the Word of God have to say about temptation? "But remember this, the wrong desires that come into your life aren't new and different. Many others have faced exactly the same problems before you. And you can trust God to keep temptation from becoming so strong that you can't stand up against it, for He has promised this and will do what He says. He will show you how to escape temptation's power so that you can bear up patiently against it" (I Cor. 10:13, *Living Letters*).

We don't know what methods God might use in making a way of escape from temptation for us, but we can be sure that one way of escape is for us to start talking to Him about the temptation. When Christ talked with His disciples in the Garden of Gethsemane, He said, "Watch and pray that ye enter not into temptation: the spirit indeed is willing, but the flesh is weak" (Matt. 26:41).

We must settle it in our hearts that God is listening. All we have to do is cry out to Him and He will deliver us. This was very clearly illustrated to me after I became a Christian and was back home with my family and in the business world again. I was out to dinner with some business acquaintances, and the other fellows had cocktails. The desire to drink was so great I broke out in a cold sweat. I cried in my heart, "Oh, God! Deliver me!"

Immediately a great peace came over me, my will was strengthened by the encouragement God gave me and I didn't yield to temptation.

AN OUTLINE FOR TALKING WITH GOD

Not long ago a fellow said to me, "I'm afraid to pray where anyone will hear me. I don't know how. I don't know what to say or how to say it."

If you feel that way, don't be discouraged. The disciples didn't know how to pray, either. They came to Jesus one day with this request, "Teach us to pray." In response, He gave them an outline for talking to God. (See Matthew 6:9-14.)

"After this manner therefore pray ye: *Our Father which art in heaven.*"

We are first directed to call upon God as our Father. When we pray that way we are calling attention to our personal relationship with Him. We are members of His family.

We alcoholics know what it means to be lonely, especially when we take the first few steps up the road to recovery. Any alcoholic has a tendency to feel as though he is the only one in the world. Yet he is never alone if God is his Father. God is always with His children and they always have access to Him.

But that is not all. We who are God's children are all members of a large family and have brothers and sisters in Christ who are willing to stand with us and help to relieve us of our loneliness.

The beginning of a successful prayer life is the recognition of our relationship to God as our Father and unshaken confidence that this relationship is a reality. Paul writes in Romans, "For His Holy Spirit speaks to us deep in our hearts, and tells us that we really are God's children. And since we are His children, then we will share His treasures—for all God gives His Son Jesus is ours now too" (Romans 8:16-17*b*, *Living Letters*).

It is wonderful to know that we can go right to the source, the very Creator of Heaven and earth—and our Creator— and receive from Him because we are His children and He is our Father.

"Hallowed be thy name."

The word "hallowed" means revered. When you revere a person you regard him with profound respect. When we pray, we go before Almighty God not only with reverence but with praise and thanksgiving. We honor His holy and wonderful and blessed name.

All of us have days when we have a heavy heart because things aren't going as well for us as we'd like them to go. When that happens, make this experiment. Start thanking God. Thank Him that you are alive and that He has made your body and, although you may have damaged it with alcohol, He has been healing and repairing your body and keeping you alive. Thank God for the beauty around you. Begin to praise Him and see what a difference it will make in your life.

Praise is the elevator that lifts us up out of the pits of despair. When we come to talk with God, we need to come with a thankful heart.

In the Al-Anon booklet *Wives and the Family Afterwards* the statement is made, "Avoid, then, the deliberate manufacture of misery. But if trouble comes, cheerfully capitalize on it as an opportunity for growth."

We must be able to pray something like this, "Lord, I thank Thee that Thou art my God. I don't understand this circumstance, but I know that You are in everything that happens to me, and I want to receive Your good from it. Praise Your Blessed Name."

"Thy kingdom come."

Christ tells us that we are to pray for the kingdom of our Father to come. God is the One who keeps this universe in its proper order. Before Him every knee will bow and every tongue will confess that Jesus Christ is Lord to the glory of God the Father. He is the final authority.

Man has rebelled against God and His authority. That is one of the difficulties of an alcoholic. He is a rebel. In his rebellion against his world, he wants to be king. If he can't be the king in the world he lives in, he'll create his own world out of a bottle.

On the road from social drinking to alcoholism, an alcoholic has developed a self-centered personality that says, "I love me and I don't love you." He has a difficult time tolerating anyone or anything that doesn't knuckle down to his warped reasoning.

To a certain extent that is true of everyone, alcoholic or not.

But the prayer Christ gave says, "Thy kingdom come." When we pray that way we are praying that He will take over the final authority in our lives. We want to make Him the King of everything that we think, or say, or do.

"Thy will be done in earth, as it is in heaven."

We alcoholics are a stiff-necked lot. It is hard for us to get to the place where we want to turn our wills over to someone else, even to God. And even after we have done it once, from time to time we revert to our former stubborn attitude of balking at God's will.

That is the reason we should daily renew the surrender of our wills to God's will. We should not walk out of our homes without having committed ourselves to our Lord and without having relinquished our will to Him so that we might do His will all during that day.

Rev. Charles L. Allen makes this statement, "Obedience to His will today means that God assumes the responsibility for our tomorrow."*

That is a challenge we alcoholics can accept.

As we start on the comeback trail, we demand the solution of all our problems *now*. And we want to know what the solution to these problems is going to be before we give in to any plan or program. That may be what we want, but frankly, I have never known it to work out that way.

The fellow or woman who is still holding out because he wants to know exactly how everything is going to end before he begins is probably still rebellious and still drinking. The person who says, "I'm giving myself over to You. Here's my will for today, make it into whatever You have for me," is the one whom God can help. For this individual He smooths out the difficult places, unites families, restores businesses, and finds jobs. God has something to work with.

"Give us this day our daily bread."

Christianity is practical. God is practical. He knows our needs and wants to supply them for us.

The Apostle Paul, writing to the Christians at Thessalonica, said "that if any would not work, neither should he eat." He also said that the man who doesn't take care of his family is worse than an infidel (I Timothy 5:8). God is love. He does not want to see our families go hungry. So He will see to it that we have the work we need. "Wherefore, if God so clothe the grass of the field, . . . shall he not much more clothe you, O ye of little faith? . . . But seek ye first the kingdom of God, and his righteousness; and all these things shall be added unto you" (Matthew 6:30-33).

If we follow the outline Christ gave us in the Lord's prayer

*God's Psychiatry, published by Fleming H. Revell Co.

we will be following the teaching of this portion of Scripture, too. We will seek the kingdom of God and His righteousness first, and then look to our material needs.

This doesn't mean that we can sit in our office with our feet on the desk or lie in bed until noon and then expect God to supply our needs. It does mean that He is going to give us the perseverance we need in looking for a job. And if we really believe He cares for us as a father cares for his children, we will not become discouraged.

Let me illustrate: You have been honestly praying according to Christ's direction in your daily devotions. You have given your all to God and are looking to Him for guidance as the King of your life. You make the rounds of the employment agencies and run down the ads on this particular day, but there is nothing for you. In spite of that, you can say in all honesty and sincerity, "Thank You, Lord. I know that You didn't want me in any of those places. But I'm not going to give up or be downhearted. I'm going to keep looking because I know that You are going to open the right door. And that is where I want to work." Such an attitude will prevent frustration and much anguish and turmoil.

When we are in the place God has opened up for us, we will have all that we need in a financial way. And if we do the job well, we will have the respect of our employer and the men with whom we work. The problems we have had before because of our selfish, alcoholic personalities will no longer be evident because God has changed our lives.

If we do have problems, we can talk with Him about them when we talk with Him each morning. We can say, "God, I'm having trouble with this job You provided for me. I want You to work it out." And He will. I can vouch for that because of my own personal experiences.

I have my own quiet time with God in the morning before the rest of the household is awake. I get out my date book and go over all of my appointments with Him, the classes I am to teach, my duties at the Mission, the radio and TV responsibilities. I get God in on everything I plan to do. Then I commit myself to Him so He can give me the wisdom and strength I need.

When I was in the business world I talked over my business problems with God in the same way. It was a thrill to see how He helped us to run our business. Before I went into the ministry God seemed to make it clear that I should live by faith, trusting Him to supply our material needs.

We had some obligations because I was still making restitution for some of the things I had done in the past. My wife and I marveled at the way God took care of us. This experience was good preparation for coming to the Mission, where we could not plan on receiving a specified amount of money each month.

Garland Thompson and his wife had four children, and my wife and I had two. There have been many difficult periods, financially, but we have seen God do some wonderful things. I shall never forget coming home one frigid February day to find my family huddled together in the kitchen. We had run out of fuel oil and had no money to buy more. My wife was trying to heat the kitchen with the gas oven.

"God didn't send us to Omaha to starve us or for us to freeze to death," we said. Knowing that we were in the center of His will and He would meet our needs, we asked God to fill that oil tank.

That afternoon I felt urged to go to the place of business that had been doing our printing. As I visited with one of the men in the office, I wondered why I was there. We didn't talk about the Mission, finances, or my empty oil tank. "Lord," I prayed silently, "please show me why I am here." After a time I excused myself to go back to the Mission.

"Wait a minute, Jerry," the man said. "Would you accept a gift?"

"The Mission always accepts money," I answered.

"I'm not talking about the Mission right now. Would you accept a personal gift?"

"Yes," I said, "if you want me to take it personally, I will."

He wrote out the check as we continued to talk about advertising and sales promotion. I didn't tell him until a long while later, but that check was for exactly the amount needed to pay for filling our oil tank. That oil tank has never been empty since.

We believed that God would supply our daily needs. He has always done so. He will do the same for you, if you make your needs known to Him and trust Him to supply them. He is always listening and wants to give us what we ask for.

"Forgive us our debts as we forgive our debtors."

When you present such a petition, you are not bargaining with God. "Lord, I'll forgive Joe, if You'll forgive me."

Christ taught that an unforgiving spirit is sin and blocks the blessing of God. One of the greatest hindrances to our full recovery as alcoholics is the lack of a right spirit toward some friend, associate, or member of our family.

I can illustrate this point by telling you about a very wealthy individual I know who has been hospitalized, psychoanalyzed, and treated with antabuse, the drug that builds a chemical fence around an alcoholic to keep him sober while he is trying to gain his footing on the road to recovery. We have dealt with this individual at the Mission, trying to help him, but he has always fallen back to drink.

"I really think he's going to make it this time," the psychiatrist who had been working with him said to me.

"I wish I could agree with you," I told him, "but I can't see him making progress. Just ask him about his sister and you'll see why."

This man has built up such resentment and anger against her that the very mention of her name sets him into a rage. God cannot deliver him from the clutches of alcohol addiction so long as he holds such hatred in his heart. He is still undelivered, and will be so long as his attitude toward his sister is one of unforgiveness.

If we ask God for something and don't see an answer, we should take an inventory of ourselves to see if some unconfessed sin is holding back God's answer. Once we do that and are confident that we are right with Him, it is good for us to remind ourselves that while God always answers prayer, He doesn't say when or how. He will answer our prayers in His own time, according to His will, and for His glory.

Someone has written, "God will give His best to those who leave the choice to Him."

"Lead us not into temptation, but deliver us from evil."

Christ is directing us in this petition to pray for victory over Satan so he will not be able to defeat us and destroy our witness and our testimony for God.

There are two great forces at work in the world today—the unlimited power of God and the limited power of Satan. Satan is out to do anything he can to overcome the unlimited power of God. He can't do this, yet he keeps trying. And, because we don't understand, there are times when we are taken in by him and his cunning.

One of Satan's attacks is along the line of tempting us to question the Word of God. He whispers to an alcoholic, "It isn't going to do you any good to pray for help in overcoming alcohol addiction. You're hooked. You can never get off the stuff."

If the devil sees that he can't draw us back into a life of drunkenness, he'll try something else. He may tempt us to take our minds off God by a selfish interest in material things.

Deceived by him, we may unwittingly go into a life of fanaticism and thus become ineffective as God's servants.

Peter tells us that Satan goes about like a raging lion looking for someone he can destroy. His attacks are varied; all have a single purpose—to try to destroy our faith and to get us to turn our back on God.

Though Satan often succeeds in his attacks against Christians, we should remember that His power is limited. He can't do anything to us unless we permit it. We can allow him to get the advantage over us in two ways: (1) by not being aware of his craftiness; (2) by deliberately yielding to his temptations.

Since we are creatures of choice, we can choose the right way or the wrong. The decision is up to us.

Satan is at work today, endeavoring in every way possible to get the advantage in our lives. If we associate with our old drinking friends and frequent places where beverage alcohol is sold, and if we neglect the Word of God, Satan will gain the advantage sooner or later and drag us down into alcoholism once more. That is the reason Christ urges us to pray daily that we will be delivered from temptation and protected from evil.

A verse in Revelation tells how a certain group of people overcame the limited power of Satan through their faith in the Lord Jesus Christ: "And they have overcome (conquered) him by means of the blood of the Lamb and by the utterance of their testimony, for they did not love and cling to life even when faced with death—holding their lives cheap until they had to die [for their witnessing]" (Revelation 12:11, *The Amplified New Testament*).

Always remember this, Christ's death was a victory over the devil. And we can be victorious through Christ Jesus our Lord. Because of His victory and our relationship to Him, we can ask, with complete assurance, that God will deliver us from the temptations of the day.

"For thine is the kingdom, and the power, and the glory for ever, Amen."

As we pray, after we have spoken of our relationship with God and have laid our entire lives and our needs before Him, we end with the acknowledgment that He is the King, and the power and the glory are to be His. The things we have talked over with God and have asked Him for are going to be done because of His merits, not because of us and our merits. The answers to our prayers will come about because Christ loved us so much that He gave Himself for us, that we might have life, and that we might have it more abundantly.

"It is of the Lord's mercies that we are not consumed, because his compassions fail not," the Prophet Jeremiah wrote. "They are new every morning: great is thy faithfulness. The LORD is my portion, saith my soul; therefore will I hope in him. The Lord is good unto them that wait for him, to the soul that seeketh him" (Lamentations 3:22-25).

3

SHARE HIMSELF

AN ARTICLE in the *Reader's Digest* ended with the following statement: "Ellen has bloomed in her work with the public-relations firm. She says, 'Yes, there is a joy in sobriety—but probably not the kind of joy most people imagine. It's a joy of being able to cope with emotional problems. I used to be frightened to get on a bus by myself! Now I take on all kinds of things. There's no sudden pride in this. The recovery of the alcoholic is the work of years. It is a complete remaking.' "*

Yes, there is much to remake.

"In the give and take of normal relationships, these men, that is, alcoholics, cannot give; they can only take from a supplier or protector," says Boston physician David J. Myerson.

In the throes of alcohol addiction the alcoholic has developed a very self-centered, antisocial personality. If he is going to make a complete reversal of his life and no longer be addicted to alcohol, he must start learning to give rather than to continue taking.

Sharing is not easy for anyone, for all are selfish and are disposed to look out for themselves first. We alcoholics are more selfish than most because we've been so concerned about

*"Women Who Drink Too Much," by Neil Gilkyson Stewart, *Reader's Digest,* May, 1962.

ourselves and satisfying our drive to drink for so long. It is
going to be very hard for us to break the pattern.

SHARE YOURSELF WITH GOD

We must recognize that we need help. We need to *want*
God to have complete control in our lives. Then we must
come to Him, frankly admitting our selfishness, and ask God
to help us. We must ask Him, by the power of His Spirit, to
enable us to show forth the giving and sharing personality of
the Lord Jesus Christ, who lives in each believer.

"Give, and it shall be given unto you; good measure,
pressed down, and shaken together, and running over, shall
men give into your bosom. For with the same measure that
ye mete withal it shall be measured to you again" (Luke 6:
38).

SHARE HIMSELF WITH OTHERS—TO RECEIVE HELP

There are many people who want to help alcoholics like
you and me, but they can't do a thing unless we ask for help.
Once we've straightened things out with God, we should go
to our families, our friends, and the church, and ask them to
help us if we haven't done so already.

We may find that it's almost impossible for us to make such
an admission—that we need help—to a wife or husband. We
don't have to start with someone so close to us, however. Our
pastor is waiting to hear us ask for help. The chances are he
knows all about our need and has been praying for us for
months.

Alcoholics Anonymous is waiting to hear from us. Their
entire organization and program is set up to help individuals
just like us.

The National Council on Alcohol has local organizations
in many cities which exist for the sole purpose of helping
alcohol addicts.

Most state and local governments have programs for our help. Even a number of large corporations like Western Electric, Allis Chalmers, and Dupont have medical programs for the treatment of alcoholism. Employers everywhere are becoming increasingly aware of the problems of alcoholics and their need for help.

If we really want to get straightened out and back on the road of sobriety and respectability, we will find many people who are ready to help us.

SHARE HIMSELF WITH OTHERS—FOR FELLOWSHIP

A couple of men who came up through our New Life Program and were on the Mission staff for a time said they didn't care to go to a certain church. They complained, "The people there just aren't friendly. They act as though they just don't want us around because we're from the Mission."

I did a little checking, and I found these men came to church late—so late they were just in time to be seated before the service began. They would ask the usher to seat them as close to the door as possible, and when the benediction was given they made a beeline for the door. Their haste would make you think someone was giving away twenty-dollar bills on the street corner!

It was true that no one spoke to them. No one had a chance to speak to them!

Fellowship is a two-way street. It must be given and received again. The only way we are going to have fellowship with other Christians is to respond when it is offered to us. A church congregation has a Christian responsibility to be friendly and to offer fellowship to those who come to worship with them. We have a responsibility to give them the chance to be friendly, and to respond to their overtures.

All too often we alcoholics feel that we have attended all the services we need when we go to a Sunday morning service.

We ought to go to Sunday school, the Sunday evening service, prayer meeting, and the men's fellowship. In addition to the spiritual help we get from such meetings, we will be given an opportunity to get better acquainted with the members of the congregation and will have more opportunities for fellowship.

Let me tell you about LaVern and his wife, Verna. After his conversion and deliverance from alcohol addiction, they started going to a different church than they had been attending. People invited them to their homes after one service or another. He gave his testimony in the church and a whole host of Christians, many of whom he and his wife didn't even know, began to pray for him.

"How can I fail," he asked humbly, "with prayer help and fellowship like that?"

When we begin to go with our family to Sunday school as well as church, the people there begin to know us as a family unit once more. They see our interest in spiritual things and realize that we are truly changed—that we have a new life.

To be sure, we may come in contact with people who will treat us scornfully for what we have been. I lost a very good Christian friend when I gave up my pastorate to go into the ministry of rescuing alcoholics. But such a loss won't be experienced often. Most Christians are excited about the fact that one who has been caught in the meshes of alcohol addiction has been freed by the Lord Jesus and is endeavoring to lead others into that same freedom. That is especially true if we make ourselves available to be used of God in the local church program.

I have never known of a person with such an attitude toward service who wasn't made welcome, regardless of church or denomination. Nor have I known one who, having given his testimony at a prayer meeting or a Sunday night service, was not greeted with warm fellowship by the people.

Let me tell you about the experience of Lloyd. When Lloyd accepted Christ as his Saviour and was restored to his lovely young wife and two children, he moved back to his hometown, but not without misgivings. "I'll never be able to get a job here," he said, "let alone be accepted by the people who know what a scoundrel I've been."

It was difficult for him to get a job and there were those who would have nothing to do with him, but he stood firm as a Christian through it all. And, longing to share his experience and the joy of his salvation, he gave his testimony at a Sunday night service.

There have been few meetings in that church like that one. The hearts of all were thrilled and an entire congregation was united solidly behind him and his wife and family. From that time on, he and Karen were surrounded by Christian fellowship and Christian friends.

Not only are churches criticized for failure to help alcoholics, but Alcoholics Anonymous receives similar criticism. For instance, I have heard men say, "I've never been able to get any help from that outfit. All they do is brag about their past drunks. They haven't done me any good."

When we hear a man say something like that, we can be sure that he is one who has never made any contribution to the meetings. He has never given a word of testimony. He has never shared with those present what God has done for him. He has never really and honestly become a part of the organization.

In our New Life Program at the Mission we see this very clearly. In fact, in our group therapy classes we can actually determine whether a given individual is going to make progress or not by his willingness to give of himself. We can be quite sure he isn't going to be successful if he doesn't share with the other fellows his needs and his progress on the road to recovery. When he leaves the program there is a good chance that he'll get into trouble with liquor and be back before long, wanting to be on the program again. His basic problem is that he is so self-centered he won't share himself and he won't receive the good things God wants to share with him.

SHARE HIMSELF—WITH MONEY

We have heard it said that the last thing to be converted about a person is his pocketbook. I've heard some say that alcoholics are the most stingy people in the world. We have never learned to give of ourselves, so we are, quite naturally, not going to give of our money, either.

Paul said of the Macedonian Church, "And this they did, not as we hoped, but first gave their own selves to the Lord, and unto us by the will of God" (II Corinthians 8:5).

In the next chapter Paul spoke on the subject of giving in greater detail: "But this I say, He which soweth sparingly shall reap also sparingly; and he which soweth bountifully shall reap also bountifully. Every man according as he purposeth in his heart, so let him give; not grudgingly, or of necessity: for God loveth a cheerful giver. And God is able to make all grace abound toward you; that ye, always having all sufficiency in all things, may abound to every good work" (II Corinthians 9: 6-8).

I have found from years of personal experience with men on our New Life Program that uncommitted money in the pocket of an alcoholic is a dangerous thing. The first big test for him comes when he gets his first paycheck. It is at this point that many a man fails. He stops off at a bar, has one drink, and is off on another drunk.

What is the reason for this?

It has been a long time since he has had some money in his pockets that isn't already spoken for, and he feels good about it—proud of it. And in his pride he grows careless again and begins to travel with a fast crowd. Before he realizes it, he has taken another drink and soon is "down the drain" again.

If we are truly concerned about making a successful rehabilitation, there are certain things we must do with our money. First, we must be cheerful givers. This does not apply only to the money we give the Lord but to all of the giving we do. God has made provision for us. We should be cheerful in managing our money in all areas of our life.

Let me illustrate by telling you about a man who had conquered the problem of beverage alcohol who used to ride with me to work. On the first of the month he would complain about the bills he had to pay. "I used to feel that way," I told him at the opportune time, "but I've changed my mind about things now. There was a time when I drank up so much of my money that I couldn't have paid my bills even if I had wanted to. Now I'm thankful I have the money and the desire to pay them. Why don't you do like I do and thank God and be cheerful about paying your bills? You'll find out that you'll have a lot more fun on the first of the month."

Next, we need to recognize that everything we have has come from God and that He is using us as a channel to perform His ministry here on earth. Therefore, we should commit ourselves and our money to God.

From the Old Testament we learn that people gave a tithe (10 percent) of their income to the maintenance of the temple, the priests, and for the care of the poor and needy, plus freewill offerings. Some industrialists give as much as 90 percent of their income to the work of the Lord. Other people limit their giving to 10 percent. And of course, there are those who feel they do God a big favor by putting a dollar in the collection plate.

We try to teach the men on the New Life Program to give

at least 10 percent of their income to God's work. The amount
we give should be according to what God has given us. We
should give freely and cheerfully because of our love for Him.

Once we have decided how much of our income to give to
the Lord, giving will not be burdensome.

But Christians do need to decide where the money can
best be used. We have an obligation to our local church to
help with the maintenance of the church buildings, the
pastor's salary, and the various church activities. Perhaps we
should next consider any radio or television ministries that
have been especially helpful to us. There may be a rescue
mission in our community. If so, they always need funds.
And certainly we would want to have a part in some foreign
mission program to help carry the good news of the gospel
to those who have never heard before.

Since there are many worthy organizations who need our
help, we should ask God to show us where to place our tithes
and offerings.

We need to establish priorities for using our money. If we
have given ourselves to God, we will make the first commitment of our money to Him. Next, we will consider the care of
our families or our personal needs—clothes, food, and shelter.
We must make sure that our household is well cared for.

Our next commitment will be for restitution. We will
make arrangements to pay back the funds we have borrowed
or stolen while we were on the downward road of alcoholism.
Such restitution is most important, as it indicates whether or
not we are truly in earnest about being right with God and
making a recovery.

Should anything be left over, as we make restitution and
reduce our debt load, we should commit our funds to some
sort of a savings program with a purpose. We must be careful
to manage our lives and our finances differently than ever
before.

It must be obvious, first to ourselves and then to those around us, that we are different—an entirely new person. This will encourage the fellowship and the cooperation from others that we so desperately need.

Share Yourself with Others—to Give Help

Helping someone else in need can be one of the greatest assets in our new life. If we can help another alcoholic to get the victory of Christ in his life and deliverance from alcohol addiction, we will find that we ourselves are that much stronger. We should witness whenever we have opportunity and take an active part in the visitation program of our church. If our church doesn't have such a program, we should encourage them to start one.

Such a program will be of great help in reaching the alcoholics in our communities. Contrary to popular opinion, most of the alcoholics are not on skid row but in our neighborhoods. The only way we can find them is to go from door to door, inviting people to church and telling of the way God has changed our lives.

We can witness and help others through the AA program. We can help to organize an Alcoholics Victorious group in our church. We can take part in the work of the local rescue mission, helping the 3 to 12 percent of men who do end up on skid row. We can tell them what God has done for us and encourage them to believe He can do the same for them.

Sharing ourselves with others will do something for us that nothing else can. It will help us to build an entirely new set of friends and will eliminate from our social lives those old drinking buddies who do not as yet want to be delivered from their alcohol addiction.

When people offer us a drink from their bottle, we should offer them a drink of the water of life, the gospel message found in the Bible. We should talk to them about God and what He has done for us. If we do, one of two things will happen. We will win them to Christ, or they will cut us out of their social affairs, which means we will have more time for our new and loyal friends who appreciate our stand for the Lord.

Remember this: We will never receive until we learn to give. When we learn to give of ourselves, our money, and our very lives, we will (according to God's Word) receive "good measure, pressed down, shaken together, and running over" (Luke 6:38). God wants to give good things to those who will share them with others.

4

LIVE A STEP AT A TIME

IT TOOK MOST OF US years to sink into the oblivion of alcohol addiction, and we probably spent years as alcoholics. It might not take an alcoholic as long to come back as it did to go down, but he must understand that rehabilitation is going to be slow and painful. The road to recovery can only be taken a step at a time.

Since alcoholism has defeated us in body, soul, and spirit, and caused a complete breakdown in our lives, we are going to have to rebuild that which was broken down.

In order to build successful lives for now and for all eternity, we must acknowledge several things: (1) that God knows the end from the beginning, (2) that He will direct our paths if we ask Him to, and (3) that we can only follow God's instructions one day at a time.

Almost nineteen hundred years ago Jesus taught the value of living a day at a time when He said to His disciples, "Take . . . no thought for the morrow: for the morrow shall take thought for the things of itself. Sufficient unto the day is the evil thereof" (Matthew 6:34).

A pastor friend of mine in counseling an alcoholic expressed the small-space-of-time concept in this way: "Just remember, life is a cinch by the inch, but it's hard by the yard."

One of the most startling things we alcoholics have to face when we begin to sober up and free ourselves from the anesthetic effect of alcoholic beverages is the realization that our bodies really are weak. We begin to have aches and pains we didn't know we had before. We may be suffering from malnutrition or any of a host of ailments that could be caused or aggravated by the way we have abused our bodies. Our physical weakness can be most discouraging if we don't understand that it is the normal reaction.

We should have a complete physical examination to discover the exact condition of our bodies and to begin a health rebuilding program. (It would be well to see a dentist, too, and get our teeth in good condition. A severe toothache can provide a strong temptation to go back to drink.) Getting our bodies restored to health can provide another bulwark against yielding to the pull of beverage alcohol. If we feel good physically, we are better equipped to throw off temptation.

Some of the strength we need to abstain can come from fully understanding our situation. We need to realize that we aren't going to feel good all the time. We are going to have normal periods in our emotional cycles as well as some high periods and some low periods. The times when we feel unusually downhearted and discouraged or unusually good can be danger points as far as taking another drink is concerned.

When we are down we are apt to wallow in self-pity until we resort to beverage alcohol. When we feel exceptionally good, we are apt to think we're big enough to control anything in the world and can take a social drink.

When we feel that the whole world is against us and everything is going wrong we should realize we are going through a low period. Everyone experiences low periods now and then. Just knowing that can help us a great deal in our fight against the urge to drink.

We shouldn't let those low periods influence us in our relationship with other people or our job. We shouldn't make important decisions or start big programs when we feel that way. Instead we should carry out only our normal daily routine.

This is a good time for us to see the other fellow's side of things in the right perspective. It is also very important that we spend extra time in prayer and rest.

If we recognize our low periods for what they are and that we are not going to be able to eliminate them, we will be able to go through them more successfully.

Those times when we feel exceptionally good can also cause us trouble. We need to have this thought deeply burned into our hearts: Regardless of how we feel at any given moment, we can never take another drink again. One drink will start building the fire that will send us back into oblivion.

When we are feeling our best we can do our best selling, our best work. We should use those periods constructively.

Fatigue is another enemy of sobriety with which the alcoholic must deal. Once we have sobered up, we want to be successful. We want to make up to our family everything we have robbed them of during our drunkenness. As a result, we may work too many hours. We push ourselves beyond our physical limits in our struggle to get ahead.

Tension, overwork and lack of proper rest can cause us to fall again. So can the failure to eat regularly.

Anyone who has worked with alcoholics knows that a good breakfast and lunch will go far toward helping the alcoholic keep down the demand of his body for another drink. To live successfully, a step at a time, the habits of the old days when we thought we could take our food from a bottle of beverage alcohol must be replaced with good eating habits.

Few men ever want a cocktail after eating cake or chocolate. If we have to fight the habit of a before-dinner drink, we should try eating a piece of chocolate candy.

Relaxing after we come home from work in the evening is another way of helping our bodies fight the craving for beverage alcohol. We should loosen our clothing and lie flat on our backs for half an hour or so. Whether or not we sleep doesn't matter. A shower, or just washing our hands and face, will be enough to wake us up and prepare us for the evening if we have to go out. And we feel much better following such a regime than we felt in the old days when we drank for strength to carry on.

The Apostle Paul had this to say of himself, "Like an athlete, I punish my body, treating it roughly, training it to do what it should, not what it wants to. Otherwise I fear that after enlisting others for the race I myself might be declared unfit and ordered to stand aside" (I Corinthians 9:27, *Living Letters*).

The late Dr. Oswald Chambers wrote, "Beware of dividing man up into body, soul, and spirit. Man *is* body, soul and spirit. Soul has no entity. It depends entirely upon the body. And yet there is a subtle, spiritual element in it. Soul is the rational description of my personal spirit in my body; the way I reason and think and work. Habits are formed in the soul, not in the spirit. And they are formed in the soul by means of the body."*

We must remember that our virtues or habits, as well as our vices and our lives, are made up of a series of habits. So, if we are going to live a new life we must change the pattern of our habits.

The Moral Foundations of Life by Oswald Chambers, published by Christian Literature Crusade (1961). See chapter on "Habit," p. 34.

So often people have the misconceived idea that once they have accepted Christ as their Saviour, everything depends upon Him.

Such an attitude is seen in the alcoholic who goes down to the corner bar praying, "Lord, deliver me from temptation." He orders a drink and sits there, figuratively expecting God to send His angels to remove the drink, somehow pick him up and set him out on the front sidewalk, thus delivering him from temptation. He sits with the drink in his hand for a couple of minutes and when he doesn't hear the flutter of angels' wings, he pours the drink down. Then he complains, "God didn't deliver me."

This attitude is so often seen in the lives of alcoholics: that the individual does not have to assume responsibility. God has to carry the entire load, and if He doesn't continually and dramatically take charge of every situation without any effort on the part of the alcoholic, he gets to thinking God doesn't care about him any more. And he goes back to the bottle.

This is just stupid alcoholic reasoning. We don't like to admit that we are Christians by choice and that God will never change that policy. He will continue to say, "Choose this new life. If you do, here is the way to live it." But our living is a matter of choice.

Oswald Chambers says, "We have to work out what God works in, and the way we work it out is by the mechanical process of habit."

So, the choices we make as we think a thing through are the habits we will form that will either make or break us. Anything and everything is possible in the way of habits. We cannot form a habit without thinking about it, Chambers goes on, but when once the pathway in the brain is formed, we can do a thing easily without thinking about it.

Spiritually, we have to learn to form habits by the strength God gives us. At the new birth we receive a new life which has the power to break all of the old habits. They can be completely dislodged by the expulsive power of a new affection. Most of us do not realize this, and we continue to obey habits which we do not need to obey.

If we are going to bring our body under control of a new life, we are going to have to do it by new thinking. New habit patterns come from new thoughts. And these new thoughts are going to have to be godly thoughts, such thoughts as described by the Apostle Paul in Philippians 4:8-9: "Finally, brethren, whatsoever things are true, whatsoever things are honest, whatsoever things are just, whatsoever things are pure, whatsoever things are lovely, whatsoever things are of good report: if there be any virtue, and if there be any praise, think on these things."

There is an orderly sequence of events in the shaping of our lives. As I think, I make choices. As I make choices, I form habits. As I form habits, I fix the direction of my life. So, if I am to live differently, I must form new habits. If I am to form new habits, I must make new choices. If I am to make new choices, I must do new thinking.

This was demonstarted very clearly in an individual who came to me for help. As a commando in World War II he had killed men in hand-to-hand combat. He had been captured, and someone had put a voodoo curse upon him. He thought the solution for his muddied life lay in beverage alcohol, and by the time I came in contact with him he had become a confirmed alcoholic.

I was working with him and his family when he had a near mental collapse. I suggested that he go to the psychiatric ward of the Veterans Hospital for treatment. In the few minutes we had together before they confined him to the ward, I told him, "God will straighten out your twisted thinking. Just claim Philippians 4:8 for your life. Think on good things, and God will renew your mind."

"Oh no," he countered bitterly. "This is the end of the line for me. I'm not giving up without a battle, but I'll never get out of here."

"God loves you," I said. "He doesn't want you to stay in a place like this. He's willing to make you new if you are willing to take His way." And when I took leave of him, I left a Testament with him with Philippians 4:8 plainly marked.

The doctors said it would be from six months to a year before they could even hope to see any change in him. Yet in six weeks he was released from the hospital and returned to society. He has been living a consistent Christian life since that day in the early 1950's.

He simply took God at His Word. He read that verse of Scripture over and over again. Whenever those terrifying memories that had been destroying him came flooding into his mind, he would read that verse of Scripture over and keep reading it until those thoughts didn't bother him any more. It wasn't long until the water of God's Word had washed his mind clean and had renewed it.

When he went before the psychiatric board of the hospital, they wanted to know how he had accomplished this renewal of his entire thought process. He took the New Testament from his pocket and held it up, saying, "This is the way I did it."

We can do the same.

We must not keep thinking of the past, either our successes or failures. We've got to think about the present; the good things that are around us now. On those good things we've got to build habits for a new life.

To fill our minds with good thoughts is not quite as simple as it sounds. We must deal with those things that cause us impure, evil thoughts. We quite likely will have to change our reading habits, and be more selective in our TV viewing.

We are going to have to saturate our minds and hearts with the Word of God. We should be very careful to start each day by reading from the Bible and to spend a certain amount of time in memorizing Scripture verses. Then when evil thoughts try to crowd in, we can counteract them with the Word.

We should also read other Christian literature—Christian magazines, biographies or autobiographies, or missionary books. Perhaps we might want to belong to a Christian book club. Such a club will regularly bring to our attention new publications in the Christian field. If the family budget doesn't allow for the purchase of many books, we can make use of our church library.

We should not get discouraged if we aren't able to get rid of all our evil thoughts in a short weekend. If we persevere, we will break the habit of wrong thinking and form the habit of thinking on good things.

The Holy Spirit is the master controller of the soul and body of each person who has accepted Christ and has received new life through Him. We must beware that we do not try to separate the physical from the spiritual. Our new life must be lived twenty-four hours of every day and seven days of every week. The Spirit of God, if we allow Him to, will stimulate our thoughts and our thoughts should stimulate our actions. We must recognize the close relationship between the physical and spiritual as we live out the new life within us.

"Don't drink too much wine, for many evils lie along that path: but be filled instead with the Holy Spirit, and controlled by Him" (Ephesians 5:18, *Living Letters*) .

If there is any verse in the Scriptures that should be easy for an alcoholic to understand, it is this one. We alcoholics know what it is to have our whole lives controlled by beverage alcohol. God's Word says that we are not to let alcohol control our lives but we are to be controlled by the Spirit of God.

Just as we used to let alcoholic beverages control every area of our lives, making us liars and cheats in order to get another bottle, so now we are to let God, through His Spirit, control our lives. We should aim to please God and honor Him in all our thoughts and actions.

If an alcoholic has difficulty in understanding what it means to be controlled by the Spirit, he should think back to the time when he was still a social drinker and saw a fellow who was overcome by beverage alcohol. He probably said, "I'll never be controlled by liquor the way this fellow is."

Yet the time came when he was controlled by liquor. How? By continuing to drink beverage alcohol. Finally he came to the place where liquor controlled him and he no longer controlled the liquor.

It is the same in being controlled by the Spirit of God. We don't understand how it can happen, but it can. All we have to do is to keep following the Spirit and yielding ourselves to God's way as revealed through God's Word. Such a life is the more abundant life Christ promised His followers.

We never know what a day will bring, but there is an answer in God's Word for every situation.

As you study the Word of God and ask the Spirit of God to teach you and lead you, you will receive direction in living a step at a time.

"May the God of peace, Himself, make you entirely clean; and may your spirit, soul and body be kept strong and blameless until that day when our Lord Jesus Christ comes back again" (I Thessalonians 5:23, *Living Letters*).

5

KEEP A PERPETUAL
INVENTORY

ONE OF THE IMPORTANT STEPS I took on the road up
from alcohol addiction was that of making an inventory of
myself. At that time I knew nothing of Alcoholics Anonymous and their fourth step which says, "Make a searching
and fearless inventory of yourself."

I had been quietly considering this new life that was mine
and had been reviewing the past. I knew how many false
starts toward abstinence and a respectable life I had made in
my own strength over the preceding years. I didn't want that
to happen again.

In my heart I knew that I was different. I was trusting the
Word of God now. My attitudes toward life and the people
were different than they had been, but I had to be sure.

The thought came to me that in the business world we
take inventory and we check sales and costs in order to determine whether we are making a profit or showing a loss. The
practical thing, I decided, would be to take a personal
inventory of myself.

I got out a sheet of paper and drew a line down the middle.
On the top of one side I wrote LIABILITIES; on the other, ASSETS.

I began to list under LIABILITIES all the things I knew were wrong with me. Facing up to myself honestly was one of the hardest things I had ever done in my life. I would sweat a little, argue with myself a little, and finally add one more fault to the LIABILITIES column.

Everyone who deals with alcoholics acknowledges that they are notorious liars. I wrote down in stark, bold characters that I was a liar. I am convinced that the moment I wrote that down I took the first step toward overcoming dishonesty in my life.

Once I had my faults listed honestly I began to write down my good qualities. That was more fun, but nonetheless exacting.

When I had completed my inventory and had checked my list carefully, I wrote a prayer at the bottom: "God, help me to overcome my liabilities and to increase my assets. Thank you." And I signed my name.

From time to time in the early years of my Christian life I would take out this inventory sheet and study it. Every now and then I had the joy of crossing out a liability or adding an asset. It was encouraging to have my spiritual inventory down on paper so I could actually see whether I was making progress. It showed me whether I was becoming more valuable to God, my family, and the community, or whether I was slipping back. My inventory was not just a one-time affair, or something I did once a year. It became a perpetual inventory.

Not long ago I was talking with a fellow about taking inventory. He thought it would be a good idea, but felt all he would have to list would be liabilities. "I'm all bad," he said. "There's nothing good about me."

It is not hard to list our liabilities. If we will be very honest with ourselves we will see in ourselves self-pity, self-justification, self-importance, self-condemnation, dishonesty, impatience, hate, resentment, false pride, jealousy, envy, laziness, procrastination, insincerity, negative thinking, vulgarity, immorality, trashy thinking, criticism. That list may not be all-inclusive, but it is long enough to stimulate one's thinking along the line of liabilities. We might be reluctant to list our assets, but there are a number of characteristics we should strive for if we want our Christian lives to be victorious: self-forgetfulness, humility, modesty, self-criticism, honesty, patience, love, forgiveness, simplicity, trust, generosity, promptness, straightforwardness, positive thinking, spiritual outlook, clean thinking, and looking for good in others.

We must be careful how we use our inventory after we have made it. If we spend too much time considering our faults we can get to the place where we can no longer face life because we are so disgusted with ourselves. This very thing can drive us back to drink.

But it is important to judge ourselves according to the Word of God: "For if we would judge ourselves, we should not be judged. But when we are judged, we are chastened of the Lord, that we should not be condemned with the world" (I Corinthians 11:31-32).

When we take a good look at ourselves and determine where we are failing, we can then make the needed changes in our lives, and not have to be judged by God.

When we see sin in our lives, we should confess our sin—agree with God that that specific act or thought or word is sin. "If we confess our sins, he is faithful and just to forgive us our sins, and to cleanse us from all unrighteousness" (I John 1:9).

And when we are forgiven and cleansed, we are once more in fellowship with God and able to receive the good things He wants to give us. However, we must keep in mind that if we are not willing to recognize the sin in our lives, God will have to chasten us because of it. He chastens those He loves in order to bring them to the place where they are willing to recognize their sin and confess it.

We have recently had contact with a man who has some real problems in his life and has come to us for help, We have pointed out the problem areas in his life. However, he isn't willing to accept these facts. As a result, he is miserable. He isn't able to receive and enjoy God's blessings. He is existing from day to day with God standing quietly by, putting the pressure on him through circumstances to bring him to the place where he will recognize his sins, confess them, and allow God to deliver him from them.

Another man did just the opposite. He was fed up with his old life—as fed up as a fellow can get. When he surrendered his life completely to God he went over his liabilities and his assets one by one, asking God to help him to live the way a Christian should. As a result, he was instantly victorious over alcohol addiction. He was restored to his family. His testimony was radiant. God also gave him the joy of leading others to Christ. He is happier than he has ever been, whereas the other fellow is more miserable.

In which pair of shoes will you be? The choice is yours.

We must understand very clearly that God does not expect us to straighten out our lives in our own power. He knows the sort of clay we're made of. All we can do—all we have to do is to recognize our liabilities, confess them as our liabilities, and allow God to move in by His power and wash us clean. He will forgive us and liberate us from sin's power. But we need to keep the channel open for His blessing.

I have found that my inventory has helped me to say no to temptations. I say when a particular temptation confronts me, "That's out of my old life. It's not a part of my new life. I'm not going to do that thing."

After I had accepted Christ as my Saviour and had been released from prison, I gave my testimony in numerous places. The Gideons made arrangements for me which kept me busy every Sunday. I also used to give my testimony a number of times during the week. I got to thinking I was an important individual. I was leading the early morning Tuesday prayer meeting when I turned to the camp president. "Now, look here, these fellows are getting me so many places to speak that I don't have a chance to spend any time with my family. The rest of them aren't doing anything. I don't think it's fair at all."

He didn't say a word to me. He just saw to it that I was never asked to give my testimony again. That went on for six or eight weeks. I began to miss the activity. I began to check myself and realized that I didn't have the warmth and zeal in my heart toward God I used to have. My devotions in the morning had become dry and I had to force myself to read the Bible and pray. As I checked up on myself, I saw that I was beginning to drift back into some of my old ways and was beginning to run with some of my old crowd.

My perpetual inventory sounded a warning, loud and clear. I had allowed pride to get the better of me. I hadn't been taking my opportunities to witness and testify for my Lord as I had said I would. Consequently I was drawing cold toward God. "God, forgive me," I prayed. "I'll testify for You every time You give me an opportunity from now on. If You will just open the doors for me again I will not refuse another opportunity." That very day my drift downward stopped. God gave me many chances to witness, and I have kept steadily at witnessing ever since.

A perpetual inventory can help each one of us to constantly measure where he stands with God. We should make an inventory of our lives and check it constantly. Such an inventory will provide guidelines to lead us into a close walk with God and help us to keep in tune with our Heavenly Father who loves us and wants to bless us with all good things.

Keeping a perpetual inventory will do something else for us. It will help us to develop our personality in such a way that we will be pleasing to our fellow men and will be acceptable in the fellowship of Christians. Not only will we have the advantage of good fellowship with our Christian friends, but we will also find doors opened for us to witness to others and show them how the power of God has changed our lives.

How can we alcoholics help ourselves? There are five ways:

1. Transfer our dependency to God.
2. Pray daily.
3. Give of ourselves.
4. Live a step at a time.
5. Keep a perpetual inventory.

Remember, keep looking up, and the Lord will bless you— just as much as you let Him.

Moody Press, a ministry of the Moody Bible Institute, is designed for education, evangelization and edification. If we may assist you in knowing more about Christ and the Christian life, please write us without obligation to: Moody Press, c/o MLM, Chicago, Illinois 60610.

SUMMARY

Dr. Wm. C. Menninger of the famed Menninger Clinic wrote, "If any other disease (other than alcoholism) affected our citizens so much, a national emergency would be declared." All around us, in our neighborhoods, in government offices, in businesses and factories, people are suffering with the problem of alcoholism.

We have written this book so the millions of alcoholics and their families and friends whom they affect so very much might better understand the problem, and might be better able to cope with this national emergency. It is our prayer that the alcoholic and those indirectly involved in the problem of alcoholism will be encouraged to know that GOD IS FOR THE ALCOHOLIC.

In closing, I would like to use a statement that was written by the late Dr. William Duncan Silkworth. "It's very wrong to consider many of the personality traits observed in liquor addicts as peculiar to the alcoholic. Emotional and mental quirks are classified as symptoms of alcoholism merely because the alcoholics have them. Yet those same quirks can be found in non-alcoholics, too. Actually, they are symptoms of mankind."*

I hope that you will see that the suggestions made for the treatment of the alcoholic are also good for everyone who is seeking his way in this confused, mixed-up world we live in. Yes, God is for the alcoholic, but God is for everyone who has a need to be delivered from himself into a new life. That includes us all.

*Dr. Silkworth was the Medical Chief of Towns Hospital and Knickerbocker Hospital in New York City. The statement was in an article in the January, 1947 *Grapevine*.

SUGGESTED READING

AA Grapevine. Issues of September, 1962 and October, 1963. Alcoholics Anonymous Grapevine, Inc., 305 East 45th St., New York, N. Y.

Alcohol Addiction and Chronic Alcoholism. E. M. JELLINEK, Yale University Press, New Haven, Conn. 1942.

"The Alcoholic Parent." *Ladies Home Journal*, October, 1962. DOROTHY CAMERON DISNEY.

An Alcoholic to His Sons, as told to HENRY BEETLE HOUGH. Simon and Schuster, New York, N. Y. 1954.

Alcoholics Anonymous Comes of Age, by a co-founder. Alcoholics Anonymous World Services, Inc., P.O. Box 459, New York, N. Y. 1957.

Alcoholism and Society. MORRIS E. CHAFETZ, M.D., and HAROLD W. DEMONE, JR. Oxford University Press, New York, N. Y. 1962.

Arresting Alcoholism. The Christopher D. Smithers Foundation, 405 Park Ave., New York, N. Y.

The Christian Case for Abstinence; 20 clergymen presenting prize-winning statements. Association Press, New York, N. Y. 1955.

The Cup of Fury. UPTON SINCLAIR. Channel Press, Inc., Manhasset, N. Y. 1962.

The Disease Concept of Alcoholism. E. M. JELLINEK. Hillhouse Press, New Brunswick, N. J. 1959.

"Don't Tell Me I Am Not an Alcoholic," *This Week* (April 26, 1959). JOHN BOIT MORSE.

Family Recovery. ROLAND BOYLE. Hornell Council on Alcoholism, Hornell, N. Y. 1962.

"From the Alcoholic 'Way of Life' to the Natural," *The International Student* (October, 1957).

Facts About Alcohol. Science Research Associates, Inc., 259 E. Erie St., Chicago, Ill.

God's Psychiatry. CHARLES L. ALLEN. Fleming H. Revell Co., Westwood, N. J. 1953.

The Greatest Force on Earth. THOMAS PAYNE. Moody Press, Chicago, Ill.

Health Shall Spring Forth. PAUL E. ADOLPH. Moody Press, Chicago, Ill. 1956.

Helping the Alcoholic and His Family. THOMAS J. SHIPP. Prentice-Hall, Inc., Englewood Cliffs, N. J. 1963.

How to Help an Alcoholic. CLIFFORD J. EARLE. The Westminster Press, Philadelphia, Pa. 1952.

Listen (September, 1962 and October, 1962). American Temperance Society, Washington, D.C.

Marty Mann's New Primer on Alcoholism. MARTY MANN. Holt, Rinehart and Winston, New York, N. Y. 1958.

New Efforts to Reach the Alcoholic. CHARLES E. MOREY. Chicago Christian Industrial League Press, Chicago, Ill. 1961.

Out of the Liquid Jungle. FAITH COXE BAILEY. Moody Press, Chicago, Ill. 1958.

Social Drinking. GIORGIO LOLLI, M.D. The World Publishing Co., Cleveland, Ohio. 1960.

To Wives and the Family Afterward. Al-Anon Family Group, P.O. Box 182, Madison Square Station, New York, N. Y.

Tomorrow Will be Sober. LINCOLN WILLIAMS. Harper & Brothers, New York, N. Y. 1960.

Twelve Steps and Twelve Traditions. Alcoholics Anonymous World Services, Inc., New York, N. Y. 1953. Also published by Harper & Row in 1963.

What Shall We Say About Alcohol? CARADINE R. HOOTON. Abingdon Press, New York, N. Y. 1960.